INFORMATION SYSTEMS DEVELOPMENT:
A DATA BASE APPROACH

COMPUTER SCIENCE TEXTS

COMPUTER SCIENCE TEXTS

Information Systems Development: A Data Base Approach

D.E. AVISON

BA, MSc, FBCS
Department of Computer Science,
Aston University, Birmingham

BLACKWELL SCIENTIFIC PUBLICATIONS

OXFORD   LONDON   EDINBURGH

BOSTON   PALO ALTO   MELBOURNE

To my Mother
Stella Avison

and the Memory of my Father
Leslie Stuart Avison

© 1985 by
Blackwell Scientific Publications
Editorial offices:
Osney Mead, Oxford, OX2 0EL
8 John Street, London, WC1N 2ES
23 Ainslee Place, Edinburgh, EH3 6AJ
52 Beacon Street, Boston
   Massachusetts 02108, USA
667 Lytton Avenue, Palo Alto
   California 94301, USA
107 Barry Street, Carlton,
   Victoria 3053, Australia

First published 1985

Phototypeset by
Oxford Computer Typesetting
Printed and bound in
Great Britain by
Hollen Street Press Ltd, Slough

British Library
Cataloguing in Publication Data

Avison, D.E.
   Information Systems Development;
   a database approach.
   — (Computer Science Texts)
   1. Electronic Data Processing
   I. Title   II. Series
   004′.024658   QA76

   ISBN 0-632-01247-1

Distributed in North America by
Computer Science Press, Inc.,
1803 Research Blvd.,
Rockville,
Maryland 20850, USA

Contents

Preface

This text is designed foremost for students of Computer Science and Business Studies who are undertaking a second course in data processing. Readers are assumed to have completed a basic course in data processing or have had practical experience in the area. The book will also be of value to managers who may be contemplating a data base path for their applications and to programmers and systems analysts who wish to know more about the role of the technologist in a data base environment.

Following the introduction (chapter 1), where the deficiencies of conventional systems analysis are discussed and readers are exposed to many of the ideas, tools and techniques described in this book, the chapter on *business analysis* (2) discusses the organisation: its goals, structure and information requirements. It also looks at the roles of the people working, sometimes reluctantly, on the information systems project and the best strategy to adopt to ensure its effectiveness.

By using techniques of *data analysis* discussed in chapter 3, a model of the organisation, known as the conceptual model, can be designed, and this model can be mapped onto a target data base. Various approaches to data modelling are described and the entity-relationship model is emphasised. This chapter also looks at relational theory and normalisation. The target model, frequently referred to as the *logical model*, can take a number of forms and chapter 4 highlights the relational, hierarchical and network views. These represent the models used by most data base management systems. These systems can use a number of methods to organise and access the data on backing storage files. These *physical storage techniques* are discussed in chapter 5. There is a separate chapter (6) which looks at the ways in which the various application systems are implemented using the data base, and *structured systems analysis and design* techniques are emphasised, along with the role of the users through *participation* and *prototyping*.

Particular *data base management systems*, the software supporting the data base, are discussed in chapter 7. The methods by which they interact with subsystems through application programs using conventional programming languages, and with users through query languages are highlighted. Some *Fourth Generation* systems, introduced in chapter 6, are described in this chapter. Consideration is given to the possibilities of *data bases on microcomputers* and *distributed data bases* in chapter 8. This chapter also looks at computer systems dedicated to data base use. These *data base machines* have been gaining in interest recently. Specific chapters are also devoted to *data dictionaries* (9) which provide information about the data base, but are now much more than merely 'data bases about data bases' and the role of the *data base administrator* (10). The data base project is likely to founder in the absence of either one of these.

Having described the objectives of the book, I wish to acknowledge its major limitation. I have not been able to look at many aspects in depth. Each part of the methodology could be the basis of a separate book or advanced course. Inevitably I have omitted much of the detail or have simplified areas in order to stress the important elements of the methodology and to emphasise its unified nature. Following each chapter is a list of references and at the end of the text a full bibliography is provided which can be used to help fill in the detail once the overall approach is understood. The Bibliography also contains a list of references to many of the hardware and software products mentioned in the text.

Each part of the methodology, each chapter of the book, could be looked upon as a piece of a jigsaw, and a failure to get each one right may cause disappointment to managers and staff of an organisation and eventual failure of the information systems and data base project. An *Appendix* is provided which describes an implementation of the methodology which was carried out at a computer service company. It attempts to draw together these pieces of the jigsaw into a unified whole.

A number of people have helped me in the writing of this text. Tom Crowe of Thames Polytechnic contributed much to the early drafts. I would also like to thank Guy Fitzgerald of the University of Warwick, Gilbert Mansell of Huddersfield Polytechnic and Bob Wood of Bristol Polytechnic for valuable help. Two referees have looked at the text before publication and they have both provided valuable guidance. I have incorporated many of their suggestions in the text. Students of Aston University have also repeatedly exposed my lack of knowledge and superficiality of thought, and I readily acknowledge my gratitude to members of our BSc and MSc courses over the last few years, and in particular to research students Paul Catchpole, Jayasri Chaudhuri, Rob Hidderley, and Hanifa Shah. Thanks also to Andrew Baker, a graduate of Aston, and Michael Coveney of Comshare for permission to publish the material given in the Appendix. Most of all I wish to thank Marie-Anne and Thomas for their kindness and support.

David Avison,
Moseley, Birmingham,
September 1985.

Chapter 1

Introduction

1.1 THE DEVELOPMENT OF COMPUTING

The early days of commercial computing were marked by great hopes but many disappointments. Business users in particular complained of broken promises. Sometimes the system was not ready when it was supposed to be operational. When it was operational, some of the features that were required were not implemented or did not work. This meant that there was a large problem in correcting and maintaining these systems. There were many reasons for these problems, but the main one was the lack of an acceptable methodology for implementing systems.

During the late 1960s, this need for a methodology was appreciated by the computing world. In the United Kingdom, the publication by the National Computing Centre (NCC) in 1968 and 1971 of their methodology for developing systems was a step in the right direction. It was also influential in the United States and elsewhere. The NCC 'package' included systems training courses and documentation tools. These helped systems analysts to follow a step-by-step methodology which would lead to the implementation of systems which **did** conform to the requirements of the users. The results of this effort helped to improve the reputation of computer people and computer applications in business.

The applications that were implemented tended to concentrate on 'computerising' manual systems. Thus the standard data processing systems, such as payroll, sales order processing and invoicing, used the computer, wherever appropriate, so as to reduce the clerical burden. In these systems the computer procedures simulated the clerical procedures and the computer files contained the same facts as their clerical counterpart. Such systems frequently gained some of the advantages that computer systems could offer, in particular those of speed and reliability.

These systems were adequate for the 1970s and reflected the technology of the time. They may well be appropriate in many smaller organisations today and in situations in larger organisations where the processes are fairly stable, because one of their main drawbacks is inflexibility. If, for example, the function changes in some way or the needs of management change, it is difficult to adapt the system to meet the new requirements. From the point of view of the user, quite small changes seem to cause immense problems to computer people. 'How easy this change would have been on the old manual system' is a cry often heard. Data processing departments spend excessive effort on maintaining systems. This frequently amounts to over 75% of their time: time that could have been spent developing new applications. Sometimes the decision has to be made to develop and implement a new system which will replace the patched up old version. But this is an expensive solution and remains appropriate only until circumstances do not change again.

Over the last few years there have been a number of developments which have made it possible to offer an alternative methodology. With data base systems, it is possible to hold the facts relating to the organisation on a data base. The 'organisation' in this context could be the whole business or a part of it, such as a division or department. Perhaps the business data base will be built up gradually, a department at a time, so that eventually the whole organisation is reflected on the data base. The various computer applications can use this as **the** data source. If the functions change, the data on the data base will probably still be appropriate. If the facts change, then the data base can be amended without affecting the application systems. There is an element of **data independence** between the data base and the applications that use it. The hardware and software can also be changed in order to reflect developments in the technology without requiring substantial changes in the application systems.

Figure 1.1 illustrates three stages in the development of data processing. In the first diagram the data is input on a document of some kind, the process carried out by the human being, and the result written down on paper. In the second diagram, the input source is the same but has been transferred to a medium which is suitable for computers to read, in this case punched cards. The process is performed by the computer which puts the result on computer output media such as line printer stationery. The system reflects the previous clerical system. Although there may well be more stages, data processing is likely to be quicker overall, due to the speed of the computer. The third diagram represents something much more radical. The facts about the business are modelled on the computer data base, and the various applications use the data base as required. If the process needs to be changed in some way, the data base will still be appropriate. The third option is likely to be the

(a) Human being as data processor.

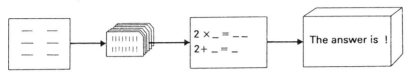

(b) The computer as data processor.

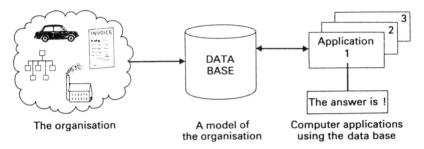

| The organisation | A model of the organisation | Computer applications using the data base |

(c) The data base approach.

Fig. 1.1 Three ways of data processing.

most rewarding, but there are risks attached to it because of the high cost and long term nature of its development.

A major problem is to construct the model of the organisation which will be held on the data base. The real world is so complex that to model the organisation, or even part of it, such as a department, is no easy task. This text proposes a methodology to achieve this aim. As Fig. 1.2 shows, the methodology has a number of phases. The first stage is to get to know something about the organisation. This business analysis is necessary so that the analysts can gain a background knowledge of the organisation, such as the goals of the firm, the management hierarchy, and the various requirements that information systems may need to fulfil.

With a background knowledge of the organisation established, it is possible to develop a conceptual model. This is a formal model of the

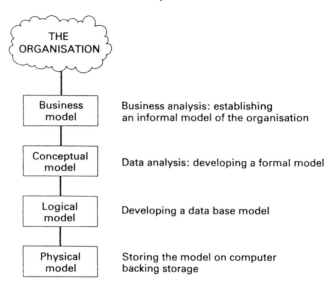

Fig. 1.2. The approach in outline (a).

organisation which is achieved by using data analysis techniques. Interviews, observation, and document appraisal, can be used to establish the basic data and data relationships, and a model is constructed of the organisation either on paper or on computer files. This model usually represents the organisation or the department modelled quite well.

The next stage is to map this model on to a computer data base. This process is usually referred to as developing the logical model. The form of this model will vary according to the data base management system (DBMS) used. The DBMS is the large piece of software controlling accesses to the data base.

Finally the DBMS maps these data structures onto computer storage media. This is the physical model which is usually held on magnetic disks and will be accessed by the various applications that require data from the data base. This access will be made using the DBMS.

The complete methodology has other aspects which are necessary for successful information systems development, and these aspects are introduced in section 1.8.

Using this methodology, the final version of the model, held on computer files, ought to be a fair representation of the organisation and should avoid some of the pitfalls, such as unnecessary data duplication, which were a characteristic of early data base use. The data base can be the basis on which to build flexible information systems providing accurate information, at the appropriate time, and at the correct level of detail for management to use for improved decision-making. It will also be used for conventional data processing tasks such as weekly payroll, sales ledger and invoicing. The data base therefore should not be seen as a 'dump for all the data in the organisation'. The data is organised so that it might be accessed by a number of different users conveniently.

Before looking in more detail at the approach adopted in this book, this chapter looks at conventional systems analysis. Section 1.2 discusses the phases of the conventional approach and the following section looks at some of the problems that may be associated with applications developed in this way. Section 1.4 looks at some of the developments in hardware and software and in other tools and techniques which pave the way for improved systems analysis. Some of the reasons for choosing a data base solution are given in section 1.5. Unfortunately early experiences with data bases and management information systems did not always prove successful, and reasons for this lack of success are discussed in section 1.6. A particular problem, highlighted in section 1.7, is the difficulty of modelling reality, that is, of representing the real world on computer files. The final section of this chapter looks in outline at the methodology adopted by this text. Although this methodology does not answer all the problems, it is hoped that the ideas, tools and techniques discussed and the use of a methodological way of proceeding are steps in the right direction.

Although this chapter discusses the opportunities open to the user of modern computing technology, it paints a rather negative picture of computing up to the 1980s. This is perhaps unfortunate because the applications were appropriate to the technology of the time. However, it is useful to appreciate the weaknesses of the conventional approach in order to understand the necessity for the methodology discussed in the text. Without such a methodology, there will be a history of failures, or at least of missed opportunities, associated with computing in the 1980s and beyond.

1.2 CONVENTIONAL SYSTEMS ANALYSIS

There have always been systems. If firms have employees, there needs to be some sort of system to pay them. If firms manufacture products, then there will be a system to order the raw materials from the suppliers, another to plan the production of the goods from the raw materials, and another to ensure that stock levels are reasonable. By 'reasonable' is meant that stocks are not so high that too much of the firm's capital is tied up in stock and not so low that there may be a stockout of the firm's products. There needs to be a system to deal with the orders from customers for the firm's products, and yet another to ensure that the products are transported, and another to send invoices to the customers and process their payments.

In the time before computers, these commercial systems were largely processed by clerical effort. The word 'largely' is appropriate, because the clerical workers would use adding machines, typewriters, and other mechanical or electrical aids to help the system run as efficiently as possible. The use of computers represents only an extension of this process. When used appropriately, computers possess advantages over clerical processing because of their speed and accuracy. If a clerical system proves inadequate in some way, a solution which involves the use of computers may well be contemplated. Data processing personnel are frequently called in to investigate applications where increasing workloads have caused strain on the clerical system, or where suitable staff are expensive and difficult to recruit, or there is a change in the type of work, or where there are frequent errors detected.

The data processing personnel may well follow the methodology recommended by the National Computing Centre (NCC) in 1968 which was revised in 1971. This approach has the following phases:

feasibility study
system investigation
systems analysis
systems design
systems development
implementation, and
review and maintenance.

These phases are frequently referred to in the literature as the systems development cycle. The use of the word 'cycle' is appropriate because at the review stage the decision could be made to start all over again. The phases are seen in Fig. 1.3.

The *feasibility study* looks at the system which is presently operative, considers its problems, and briefly looks at a range of alternative ways of doing the job. The list could include improved clerical systems as well as computer solutions. For each of these possibilities, a list of the costs and benefits is compiled and a 'recommended solution' presented to management. They will decide whether to follow this recommendation

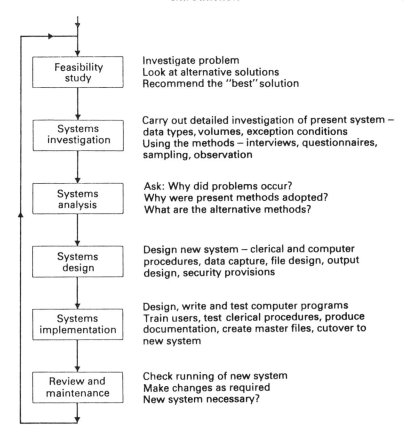

Fig. 1.3. Conventional systems analysis — the systems development cycle.

or to adopt another solution. Management will base this decision on the feasibility report along with a verbal presentation by the systems analyst.

The next stage is a detailed fact finding or *systems investigation* phase. This aims to find out the objectives of the present system and whether these are being achieved, the range of data types and the volumes of data that have to be processed, exception conditions, and the problems associated with the present working methods. These facts are obtained by interviewing personnel (both management and clerical staff), sending out questionnaires, observing the area of interest, sampling, and looking at the records that are kept in the department or records of any previous investigation work that has been compiled. The

NCC approach uses a number of documentation aids which help to ensure that the investigation is thorough.

Armed with the facts, the systems analyst asks why any problems occurred, why certain methods of work were adopted, considers whether there are alternative methods, and decides on the likely growth rates of data. This *analysis* phase leads to the design of the new system. Although usually similar to the design accepted at the feasibility study stage, the new facts may lead to the analyst adopting a rather different design to that proposed at that time.

The *design* stage involves both the computer and clerical parts of the system. The design document will contain details of the input data and how the data is to be captured (entered into the system), the outputs of the system, the processes involved in converting the input to the output and the structure of the computer and clerical files which may need to be referenced in the system. Again, the NCC methodology provides documentation tools with which to detail the input, file and output formats, and to chart the procedures. Other features of the design will be the specification of the security and backup provisions to be made, and the systems testing and implementation plans.

The next stage is to *implement* the new system. If the design includes computer programs, these have to be written and tested. Staff in the user department need to use the system and any difficulties experienced need to be ironed out. If the system is not fully tested at this stage there might soon be a loss of confidence in it because users will find errors in the system when it becomes operational. This is likely to reduce its effectiveness. Manuals for the operations staff and the user staff will be produced and the live data, that is real data, will be collected and validated so that the master files can be set up. Once all this has been carried out, the new system can be operated and the old one dispensed with. Frequently there is a period of 'parallel running' until there is complete confidence in the new system.

The final stage in the systems development cycle occurs once the system is operational. There are bound to be some changes necessary and some data processing staff will be set aside for *maintenance*. Their job will be to ensure the efficient running of the system and to make the changes required by the users. At some stage there will be a *review* of the system which will check that the system conforms to the requirements specified at the feasibility study stage, and the costs have not exceeded those predicted. A report should be produced. Sometimes the system has veered from the requirements definition significantly or new requirements have come to light and it may be sensible to consider whether it should not be replaced by yet another new system. The cycle will then come full circle as a new feasibility study gets under way.

This traditional systems development cycle has a number of features to commend it. In particular, the use of documentation standards ensures that the proposals are complete, and that they are communicated to systems development staff, the users in the department, and the computer operations staff. Further, the systems analyst ought to ensure that all the staff involved are trained to use the system in good time. The documentation aids this process as well. The methodology also prevents, to some extent at least, missed cutover dates and unexpectedly high costs and lower benefits. Early computing had a track record of these problems.

This conventional approach to systems analysis has a good track record, and it is still appropriate for many applications. But computer applications that have been implemented during this time have also had their limitations. Some of these limitations may stem from the way that the methodology is used or from the abilities of the analysts involved, but others stem from the methodology itself. Before discussing the alternative methodology suggested in this book, we will look at the problems of the conventional approach to systems analysis as represented by the early NCC methodology.

1.3 PROBLEMS WITH THE CONVENTIONAL APPROACH

The criticisms of some of the computer applications that are developed using the conventional approach include:

Failure to meet the needs of business
Inflexibility
User dissatisfaction
Problems with the documentation
Incomplete systems
Application backlog
Maintenance workload

This section looks at each of these problems which can occur in data processing applications.

As Fig. 1.4 shows, although systems that are developed by this approach can successfully deal with operational processing, such as sales order processing and the various accounting routines, there is a *failure to meet all the needs of business*. In particular, middle management and

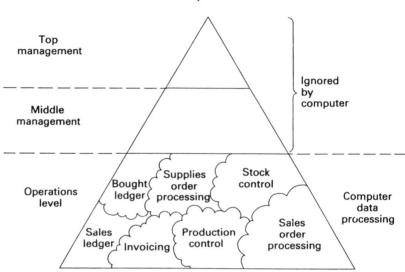

Fig. 1.4. Failure to meet all needs of business.

top management are being largely ignored by computer data processing. Management information, such as the information required to make decisions about where to locate a new factory or which product range to stop producing or what sales or production targets to aim for, is being largely neglected. The computer is being used only for routine, repetitive tasks. Managers and computers are not mixing — apart from the 'lip-service' required to sanction the expenditure necessary to buy and develop mainframe computer systems. There is now a growing awareness amongst management that computers ought to be helping them more directly.

Another major problem is the *inflexibility* of the systems that are being implemented. Computer systems are very often replacing clerical systems which are proving inadequate. However, apart from using a new technology, their designs are similar to those of the existing system. They are not intended to be adaptive: they are expected to parallel existing systems. Inflexibility also occurs for another reason. The output of the new system is decided early in the systems development process. As Fig. 1.5 shows, the design of the new system is 'output driven'. Once the output is agreed with user management, the other aspects of system design begin to fall into place. The development process may take some months to complete, and it is common and not unreasonable for users to require a change in the outputs even before the new system is operation-

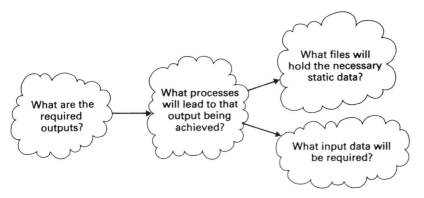

Fig. 1.5. Design is output driven.

al. But because the system has been designed from the output back-wards, such changes may necessitate a very large change in the whole system design. This can cause either a serious delay in the implementation schedule or an operational system that is unsatisfactory from the start.

User dissatisfaction therefore is a feature almost inherent in some computer applications. Frequently they are rejected as soon as they become operational. The user may have agreed the design of outputs with the systems analysts, but it is only when the system is operational that he sees the repercussions of his decisions. Many data processing departments expect the users to 'sign off' their requirements at an early stage in the development of the system. At this time the users do not have the information to agree the exact requirements of the application. They may sign the completed NCC documents which are not designed with the user in mind. On the contrary, they are designed for the systems analysts, operations staff, and programming staff who are involved in developing the system. Users cannot be expected to be familiar with the technology and its full potential. How can they usefully contribute to the debate? As a consequence, they are frequently disillusioned with computers and fail to cooperate with the systems development staff. Because of this, computer people find user staff 'bloody minded' and unable to make a decision.

In section 1.2, one of the benefits discussed of the NCC approach was the documentation standards that were an integral part of that methodology. But there are *problems with the documentation*. The orientation of the documentation, as we have already seen, is towards the technologist and not the future users of the system. The main purpose of documentation is to aid communication. A technically oriented design is not ideal for this purpose. A further problem that occurs is that the forms tend to be completed rather reluctantly by the programmer or analyst. Completion is probably required by the data processing department, but it is infrequently done well and is rarely updated as modifications to the system are implemented either as part of the development process or when maintaining the system. This makes the documentation useless because it cannot be relied upon as an accurate reflection of the true system.

Computers are particularly good at processing a large amount of data quickly and accurately. They excel where the processing is the same for all items. Here the processing is structured, stable and routine. The unusual conditions, commonly known as exception conditions, are frequently ignored in the computer system and this leads to *incomplete systems*. The exception conditions are expensive to cater for. If they are diagnosed in the system investigation stage, then clerical staff may be assigned to deal with these exceptions. Frequently they are detected too late as the systems analyst finds out exactly what 'Joe Bloggs does in the corner'. He deals with the customer who is different to the rest and has to be dealt with separately. The new system, not catering for these special circumstances, crashes soon after the system is operational.

A further problem is the *application backlog* found in data processing departments. There may well be a number of applications waiting to be developed. Some users may have to wait two or three years before the development process can get under way and a further year before **their** system is operational. The temptation then will be to offer a 'quick and dirty' solution, particularly if the deadline set for cutover proves to be somewhat optimistic. It may be politically expedient to patch over a bad design rather than spend time on good design. However, poorly designed systems will be difficult to maintain and in many businesses the *maintenance workload* is over 75% of total data processing workload.

1.4   ANSWERS TO THESE PROBLEMS

Over the last few years, a number of developments have been made. Advances have occurred in hardware, software, tools and techniques, and in the demands of managers and other users. These advances, which have enabled improvements to be incorporated in the conventional approach to data processing, have also enabled alternative methodologies to be developed which may be more appropriate in some circumstances. The improvements that are most relevant to the methodology described in this text are shown in Fig. 1.6.

Although this text is about implementing better systems for the user, such developments would not be possible but for the massive advances in hardware and software which seem to be a continuous state of affairs.

HARDWARE DEVELOPMENTS
* Data communications
* Microcomputers
* Data base machines

SOFTWARE DEVELOPMENTS
* Real time operating systems
* Data base management systems
* Data dictionaries
* Application program generators and other fourth generation tools

TOOLS AND TECHNIQUES
* Data analysis
* Relational theory
* Structured analysis and design
* Prototyping

'PEOPLE' DEVELOPMENTS
* Participation
* Management requirement

Fig. 1.6. Developments in computing.

It is very difficult to keep up with the pace of change. Access times, memory size and reliability have all changed continuously and to the benefit of the user. Costs, for any particular computing power, have also shown a general movement downwards. The flexibility and power of the software now available also provides a necessary backcloth to the developments that are discussed in this text. Developments in data communications, microcomputers, dedicated data base machines, operating software, data base management software, and data dictionaries gain emphasis here only because of their special relevance to data base implementation. The tools and techniques discussed, together with these technological developments, form the basis of the methodology. Data analysis, relational theory, structured systems analysis and design, and prototyping, are highlighted because the use of these will improve the likelihood of the data base project being successful.

The 'people' developments are also crucial. The willingness of non-computer people to become involved and contribute to the process of change, and management's will to demand these changes, also contribute positively. They are factors which are important in any computing project, but are particularly important in the long term and high cost projects discussed in this text. This section will look briefly at all these developments, but they will be re-introduced in the context of the overall methodology later in the text.

Data Communications: The ability for computers to 'talk' to each other is now commonplace, even where these computers and their associated equipment are very different and made by different manufacturers. It has opened up many possibilities for users. It has facilitated the passing of information between users. It has also allowed data of all descriptions to be held in one place (the data base) and accessed by a number of users in remote sites. Although access will sometimes be made to the central computer and data base by users in the same building, very often the users are situated in other buildings, other towns, and other countries. Figure 1.7 shows part of the EEC Network. With the development of microcomputers, Local Area Networks (LANs) are being set up

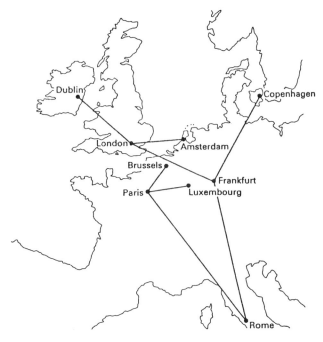

Fig. 1.7. Part of the EEC network.

within businesses which facilitate the sharing of data. A typical arrangement is shown as Fig. 1.8. In this LAN, the network is arranged as a ring structure. Alternatively the network can be arranged as a straight line and the various devices are attached to that line sharing all its facilities.

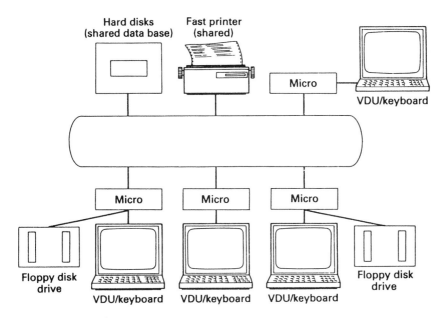

Fig. 1.8. A local area network (LAN) arranged as a ring.

Microcomputers: Microprocessors and associated technology have developed computers costing a few hundred pounds which are more powerful than many mainframe computers of the 1960s and 1970s which cost tens of thousands of pounds. They are also, by comparison, very small and some are fairly portable. Typically, they can be placed on an office desk. Some come with packages which can perform word processing, file management, spreadsheet and graphics applications. One of their most important effects is to make every office worker and manager aware of computing. This awareness is a prerequisite for successful systems implementation. Further, microcomputers can be connected to mainframes by data communications facilities. This means that the microcomputer can be used for the day-to-day work of the office, but the facilities of the mainframe can be brought in when needed. One of these facilities will be the corporate data base. Figure 1.9 is an extension of Fig. 1.8 which includes mainframe access.

Data Base Machines: Most data base systems are implemented on conventional computers. The mainframe computer represented in Fig. 1.9 will be a computer that is used for many applications, some of which use the data base and others which do not. With conventional hardware, data is located on disc by its address. This is a physical location which could have been calculated from its position in relation to the beginning of the file or its position relative to other data in the file. However, data base applications usually require data to be located by content. The user may want details of those customers who order a particular product range, or those employees who are trained in a particular technique, or, more simply, to find the record of the product 'where name = widget'. Dedicated data base hardware has recently been developed which can locate data directly by its content. This feature and others which 'optimise' the system for data base use speed up data base access significantly. These data base machines include the Britton-Lee IDM500 and the ICL CAFS.

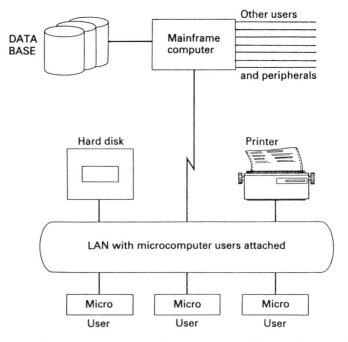

Fig. 1.9. LAN users connected to mainframe computer facilities including data base.

Real-Time Operating Systems: Without multi-user and real-time operating systems, the applications discussed in this text would not have been possible. Such operating systems are now well established: indeed it is rare for operating systems to be single user, except in a microcomputer environment. Some mainframe computer systems are capable of processing many programs at the same time and handling a few hundred users connected to the computer. Some application systems will be real-time, that is, changes to the 'real world' will be reflected in the computer files almost immediately. The response time for the operating system to react to input is therefore very fast. Conventional application systems were designed for batch processing, that is, the data for a system was batched, input, and processed together through the various programs. The application system could take an hour or more to process all the data. Frequently jobs were left overnight for processing on the computer. This processing time is not good enough for many applications.

Data Base Management Systems: A data base is an organised and integrated collection of data. A large collection of books owned by the local council is not a public library. It only becomes one when, amongst other things, the books have been catalogued and cross-referenced so that they can be found easily and used for many purposes and by many readers. A data base is also expected to be used by a number of users in a number of ways. In some companies the whole organisation is modelled on a data base, so that users can find out any information about the organisation by making enquiries of the data base. Strategies for data base use are discussed in section 2.6. There needs to be a large piece of software which will handle the many accesses to the data base. This software is the data base management system (DBMS). The DBMS will store the data and the data relationships on the backing storage devices. It must also provide an effective means of retrieval of that data when the applications require it, so that this important resource of the business, the **data resource**, is used effectively. Efficient data retrieval may be accomplished by computer programs written in conventional programming languages such as Cobol and Fortran accessing the data base. It can also be accomplished through the use of a query language which is designed for use by people who are not computer experts. These arrangements are shown in Fig. 1.10. DBMS have other facilities which are discussed later in the text. Experience with data bases has not always been successful. This has been partly due to faults in the design and implementation of the hardware and software which have been largely corrected. Another reason is the lack of a coherent methodology for implementing these systems and a failure to consider some of the wider issues. The methodology discussed in this text aims to reduce the possibility of these failures recurring.

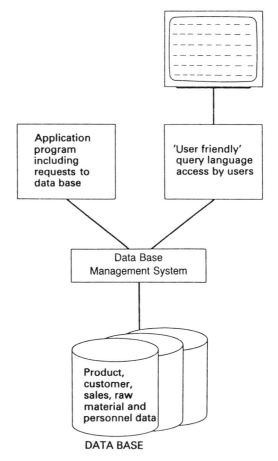

Fig. 1.10. The role of the data base management system (DBMS) intercepting the data requests of application programs and users.

Data Dictionaries: Following the library analogy used in the previous paragraph, a data dictionary represents the catalogue. In other words, it is the directory showing what data is in the data base. It will have information on each item of data held on the data base, such as its name on the data dictionary, who uses it, who updates it, and how it is validated. The dictionary is therefore crucial to the success of the data base project. Data dictionary systems can support a number of other facilities. These are discussed in chapter 9.

Application Program Generators: One of the problems mentioned in Section 1.3 was the application backlog. Writing programs in conventional programming languages such as Fortran and Cobol can be slow. Recently a number of program generators and other **Fourth Generation Systems** (see sections 6.5 and 7.6) have been developed which speed up the process of developing systems. Program generators may have a set of powerful instructions which take the place of a number of Cobol instructions. Some generate the equivalent Cobol code from a library of subroutines. An alternative method is for the user to state his requirements by filling in a form (usually a soft copy form on a VDU screen). Development time is shortened, and although the code generated may 'waste' computer power, this may not be of prime concern, because it optimises on 'people power'. These systems may also be used as prototyping tools.

Data Analysis: The development of techniques of data analysis have helped to understand the structure and meaning of data in organisations. Data analysis techniques can be used as the first step of extrapolating the complexities of the real world into a model that can be held on a computer and be accessed by many users. The data can be gathered by conventional methods such as interviewing people in the organisation and studying documents. The results are usually represented by a set of tables, known as relations, and data relationships between these relations. A number of documentation and pictorial aids also help in the process of data analysis. Some of these documents can be used as source documents for the data dictionary. The end result of data analysis can be mapped onto a DBMS. The techniques of data analysis are described in chapter 3. Readers should be aware, even in this introductory stage, that modelling the organisation on a computer data base is not easy. The whole organisation is too large as there will be too many things to be modelled. It takes too long and does not achieve anything concrete like an information system. Managers want tangible results fairly quickly. In any case it is impossible to be totally objective and our task is rather to model a particular view of the organisation, one which proves reasonable and accurate for most applications and users.

Relational Theory: As Fig. 1.11 shows, relations are tables of data. An organisation can be represented by a number of these relations. As well as being an end result of data analysis, the model is readily understood by computer people and can be interpreted by some DBMS packages. As far as the user is concerned, a relational DBMS is one which sees the data base as a collection of tables and provides a language to manipulate these tables. The model is also readily understood by people who are not computer experts. This could not be said of the equivalent file

RELATION NAME: ORDER

NAME	PART-NO.	QUANTITY
Lee	35	120
Deene	38	18
Smith	30	9
Lee	57	20

RELATION NAME: COURSE

COURSE NO.	COURSE NAME	LEVEL	YEARS	STRUCTURE
B74	Computer science	BSc	3	Full-time
B75	Computer science	BSc	5	Part-time
C30	Computer science	MSc	1	Full-time
D70	Business studies	B.A.	3	Full-time
D75	Business studies	M.B.A.	1	Full-time

Fig. 1.11. Relations, the tabular representation of data.

structures used in conventional systems analysis. So as to make the relations useful as a basis for modelling, certain rules are applied to them. These are collectively known as the rules of normalisation. Relations can be manipulated conveniently by computer programs. Certain aspects of two or more relations could be combined to highlight related sets of data or separated to highlight certain columns or rows which are of particular interest to the user. These requests to manipulate relations may be made by users who have access to a relational DBMS via a query language.

Structured Systems Analysis and Design: Just as data analysis is a series of techniques to develop a data model, there is a parallel need to understand the functions that will be applied to the data base when it is implemented. There has also been a series of improvements here, particularly the techniques which together form the basis of structured systems analysis and design. These techniques include the use of diagrammatic aids such as data flow diagrams and decision trees, and other techniques such as 'Structured English'. As can be seen from Fig. 1.12, Structured English can be very like a computer program but users can understand it because it has a simple vocabulary. The essential feature of these structured techniques is functional decomposition, that is the breaking down of large complex systems into smaller, more

```
CREDIT RATING POLICY
─────────────────────

IF the customer is a trade customer
        and IF the customer is customer for 5 or more years
                THEN credit is accepted up to £5000
        ELSE credit is accepted up to £1000
ELSE (the customer is a private customer)
        SO: no credit is given
```

Fig. 1.12. An example of structured English.

manageable and understandable subsystems. Many of these techniques have been incorporated into conventional systems analysis and have greatly improved its effectiveness. The techniques help in understanding the real-world processes and in communicating the knowledge acquired. Users can follow the analyst's documentation and confirm the analyst's understanding of the processes. Once there is agreement, the results can be readily converted into computer procedures.

Prototyping: We have seen that many systems are implemented and then rejected by the users. One way to minimise this risk is to develop a prototype first. The users can see, using this 'quick and dirty' solution, what the outputs will be like. User ideas to improve the proposed system can be incorporated into the prototype until the user finally gives his approval. At this stage the operational system can be developed with the analysts more confident that it is likely to be accepted by the users and therefore be successful. A number of computer aids are now available, such as program generators, report generators, and screen painters, which facilitate the quick production of the prototype system. These tools could be available in a Fourth Generation Package. Prototyping can also be incorporated into conventional systems analysis as an improved systems investigation technique. In some data processing departments, once the user is satisfied with the prototype, it is assumed to be operational. However there are maintenance and other problems with this approach, because it is difficult to build into the prototype the features necessary for it to be a reliable operational system.

Participation: This is a practical philosophy aimed at providing solutions to user problems. In conventional systems analysis, the importance of user involvement is frequently stressed. However it is the technologist

who is making the real decisions. The user, the person who will hopefully gain from the new system, frequently feels resentment about this lack
of true involvement. When the system is implemented, the analyst may
well feel pleased with the system, the users may not. If the users
participated more in the design and development of the system, perhaps
playing the leading role in the design, they are far more likely to be
committed to the system once it is implemented. The role of computer
analysts may then become more of a 'facilitator' than of designer, as
their role will be to advise on the possible alternatives open to the users.
The users may also try application packages rather than expect the data
processing department to develop their own designs. Another possibility is to develop a prototype which will help create the specification of
the new system.

Management Requirement: In the past, top management have often
avoided contact with computer systems. They have probably sanctioned
the purchase of computer hardware and software but have not involved
themselves with their use, rather keeping themselves at a 'safe' distance
from it. This cannot help the goal of implementing successful computer
applications being achieved. Managers need to participate in the change
and this will motivate their subordinates. Attitudes are changing,
however. There is a growing awareness about computers and most
managers will have used microcomputers in some way and can see that
more sophisticated computer systems can be used to help them in their
decision-making. Earlier computing concerned itself with the operations
of the firm. Modern computer applications concern themselves with
decision-support as well. Top management and middle management,
previously ignored by the computer (see Fig. 1.4), are being helped by
applications called decision-support systems or management information systems. These systems are backed up by the data base. Without
these systems, firms will lose out to their competitors. One possibility is
to connect the manager's microcomputer to the mainframe information
system with its data base. Managers are now far more likely to demand
sophisticated computer applications and play a leading role in their
development. This will provide the clear sense of direction necessary for
all large-scale projects.

1.5   WHY DATA BASES?

The data base provides the data resource for the organisation. The Data
Base Management System (DBMS) is the software which manages this

resource. Data bases did not gain widespread use in the United Kingdom until the middle 1970s, although DBMS were available before 1970. The systems available then were, by today's standards, somewhat rudimentary. However there were early versions of the data base packages IMS, IDS and Total which are still available.

In the 1970s, a number of large firms with mainframe computers adopted the data base approach. There were a number of reasons, for example to:

Reduce data duplication and inconsistency and consequently increase its shareability

Increase the integrity of the data

Increase the speed in implementing systems

Ease file access by programmers

Increase data independence

Provide a management view of the organisation

Improve the standards of the systems developers

Reduce data duplication: Large organisations, such as insurance companies, banks, local councils, and manufacturing companies, had for some time been putting large amounts of data onto their computer systems. Frequently the same data was being collected, validated, stored and accessed separately for a number of purposes. This 'data redundancy' is costly and can be avoided, or at least reduced, by the use of a DBMS. (In fact some data redundancy is reasonable in a data base environment, but such redundancy should be known and controlled.) If the data is collected only once, and verified only once, there is little chance of inconsistency. With conventional files, the data is often collected at different times and validated by different validation routines, and therefore the output produced by different systems could well be inconsistent. With reduced data duplication, data can be shared but it is essential that good integrity and security features operate in such systems. Furthermore, each application should run 'unaware' of the existence of others using the data base. The computer system must therefore be powerful enough that performance is good even when there are a large number of users concurrently accessing the database.

Increase data integrity: In a shared environment, it is crucial for the success of the data base system to control the creation, deletion and update of data and to ensure its correctness. Furthermore, with so many users accessing the data base, there must be some control to prevent failed transactions leaving the data base in an inconsistent state. Again, there must be proper mechanisms to control access by unauthorised users. Although these aspects represent challenges, they also represent an opportunity to increase data integrity and security significantly. These requirements will be easier to effect in a data base environment than one where each application sets up its own files, because of the possibilities of central administration. Standards need only be agreed and set up once for all users.

Increase speed of implementing systems: Systems ought to be implemented in less time, since systems development staff can largely concentrate on the processes involved in the application rather than on the collection, validation, sorting, and storage of data. Much of the data required for a new application may already be held on the data base, put there for another purpose. Accessing the data will also be easier because this will be handled by the data manipulation features of the DBMS.

Ease file access by programmers: Early DBMS used well-known programming languages such as Cobol and Fortran as the language which was used to access the data base. Cobol, for example, was extended to include new instructions which were used when it was necessary to access data on the data base. These 'host language' extensions were not difficult for experienced computer programmers to learn and to use.

Increase Data Independence: Data independence is the ability to change the format of the data or the medium on which the data is held or the data structures without having to change the programs which use the data. Conversely, it also means that it is possible to change the logic of the programs without having to change the files. This separation of the issues concerning processes from the issues concerning data is a key reason for data processing departments opting for the data base solution. It makes changes much easier to effect, and therefore provides for far greater flexibility.

Provide a management view: With conventional systems, management is not getting the benefits from the expensive computing resource that it has sanctioned. At the same time, managers were becoming aware of the need for a corporate view of their organisation. Such a view requires data from a number of departments, divisions, and sometimes companies in a larger organisation. This corporate view cannot be gained if files are established on an applications basis and not integrated as in a data base. With decision-support systems using the data base, it becomes possible for problems previously considered solvable only by intuition and judgement to be solved with an added ingredient, that of information. Some of this information could be provided on a regular basis whilst some will be of a 'one-off' nature. Data base systems should also respond to this type of request.

Improve standards: In traditional systems development, applications are implemented by different project teams of systems analysts and programmers and it is difficult to apply standards and conventions to run for all applications. Computer people are reputed to dislike following the norms of the firm, and it is difficult to impose standards where applications are developed piecemeal. With a central data base, it is possible to impose standards for file access and update and to impose good privacy and security features.

1.6 EARLY DATA BASE EXPERIENCE

Unfortunately not all the ambitions discussed in the previous section were realised in the early years of data base systems. Data was frequently collected, input and validated more than once; sometimes data retrieval times were slower than those of conventional file access; the integrity and security of the data bases were called into question; some data base systems only supported batch processing and limited file handling facilities; and it was frequently difficult to incorporate new data structures without causing problems, which sometimes required the time-consuming process of reorganising the data base. Data base projects were very large and complex and the technology was not well understood. In short, the claims of the approach were not being substantiated.

Worse, this proved to be an expensive venture. The DBMS software was expensive, the extra hardware required to support it was expensive, and the conversion of existing systems was also expensive. Organisations adopting the data base approach were frequently surprised by the extra main memory required to hold the data base software and the extra handling routines to support it. Frequently it was necessary to spend large sums of money on backing storage, much of which were needed for overheads consumed by the DBMS, not for the company's data. Further, the data base environment is a complex one. It requires sophisticated programming, backup and recovery procedures and the computing installation becomes increasingly vulnerable in the event of failure.

There were a number of reasons for early problems with data base systems. They included:

Limitations of the software

Limitations of the hardware

Inexperience with the technology

The lack of a data dictionary

The lack of a data base administrator

Poor user languages

The lack of management committment

The difficulty of modelling reality

Limitations of the software: Some data base systems were unable to express the complex logical structures of the data found in the applications. IMS, for example, saw data relationships only in terms of hierarchies and had limits on the number of files that it could handle. Some of these limitations have been corrected in later versions of the system and in alternative packages, but proved a significant obstacle to successful implementation of data base systems at this time.

Limitations of the hardware: On implementing the DBMS software it was soon realised that it would be necessary to upgrade the hardware. In other words to gain the advantage of the approach, it was necessary to purchase extra disk capacity and sometimes to upgrade the computer itself with extra internal memory or a more expensive computer in the series. These monies may well not have been set aside by management who may be unwilling to invest further on the DBMS project until it 'proves' itself. Without this extra hardware, this may be particularly difficult to achieve.

Inexperience with the Technology: Systems development staff, that is programmers and systems analysts, were inexperienced with the data base technology and therefore had problems converting old systems to the new technology and in developing new ones. Computer people have a reputation for experimenting at the expense of the user. Attempts were made to implement systems using the new technology before the technologist was fully conversant with that technology.

The lack of a data dictionary: The need for a data dictionary was infrequently recognised and they were not normally provided with the data base system. This meant that it was difficult for users to know what was already in the data base and consequently difficult to avoid unnecessary data duplication and, in general, to control data base use.

The lack of a data base administrator: The need for a data base administrator was also not recognised. Standards for data base use were rarely imposed, conflicting requirements of users unsatisfactorily resolved, and the performance of the data base system rarely monitored, so that few steps were made to improve performance. If such a role had been created, there were few facilities, such as data dictionaries, that would help the task being fulfilled successfully.

Poor user languages: Access to the data base was gained through a host language rather than through the use of a query language. Host languages are suitable for computing professionals. It was therefore not possible for the users of the company to access the data base themselves. Some of the expected gains of the data base approach would only accrue if there was access to the data base available to less experienced users. Non-procedural, natural language-like query languages only became generally available in the late 1970s.

Lack of management committment: It was not usual for managers to become involved in computing. Computers were for experts, and, as we saw in the previous paragraph, there were no 'user-friendly' query languages available for data base access on most systems. The data base applications therefore continued to concentrate on operations level processing rather than on decision-support systems.

The difficulty of modelling reality: It is difficult to accurately reflect the organisation onto computer files. How does the systems analyst hold on computer files the facts that represent the organisation? Without this being achieved, it is likely that the applications on the data base will be incomplete and inaccurate. This was a difficult problem in the early days of data bases and the problem is still with us.

1.7 THE DIFFICULTY OF MODELLING REALITY

Most of the problems discussed in the previous section have been overcome. The technology has improved out of all recognition, and this applies to both hardware and software. Costs have continued to go down, whilst both capacities and speed of access improve. The technologist has learnt how to use the computer data base environment to the good advantage of the company. 'User friendly' languages have been developed so that those users who are not computer experts may profitably access the system themselves. Managers are more involved with computing, partly as a result of their use of microcomputers. Data dictionary systems have been developed which interface with the data base packages and most companies that use data base systems have employed a data base administrator. The final problem remains with us: how to model the real world onto a data base.

A data base can only be 'A' and *not* 'THE' model of the organisation. It cannot reflect reality completely and accurately for all purposes. It aims to be a reasonable reflection of the organisation which is useful for most purposes. It may present a distorted picture for some purposes. Even if the modelling process has 'gone according to plan', the resultant data base cannot be perfect. No data model can be 'objective' for all purposes: the modeller is not objective. We can never fully know reality; our view of the real world is distorted by the perceptive process.

We are aiming to produce the best model of the organisation that we can, and use it as a data base for our applications. This is difficult. The data on the data base will be used by many applications and therefore it is important that it is well validated. However, no data can be guaranteed 100% accurate. It may be 'accurate enough' for some applications, but it will not necessarily be good enough for new applications which are added to the data base later. The cost of ensuring 100% accuracy for all applications would be too prohibitive.

Another problem of which the reader ought to be aware is that in aiming to model the organisation, we are making a number of dubious assumptions. The data collected may not necessarily be useful at a later date. This is an expensive overhead on an already expensive enterprise. If it might be useful in the future, the data may then be out-of-date. Like many an attic, the data base may contain a lot of rubbish. Utopian data bases therefore do not exist. We are attempting to achieve that which proves useful for most demands. In order to achieve this we need a positive methodology.

This text aims to provide such a methodology, one that will harness some of the most sophisticated aspects of the new technology. It looks at the documentation techniques, the role of the innovator, and the role of the manager, for, without considering all aspects of the processes and the people involved, the data base project will fail ... and it will be a most expensive failure. There are a number of stages in the methodology. These are stages in developing a data model which is almost natural to the user (**conceptual model**) and through a series of mappings transfer it to a model which is natural to the machine (**physical model**). By 'natural' we mean understandable. These different views are necessary because it is not reasonable to expect a particular view to be natural to both man and machine. A brief introduction to the steps in the methodology is given in the next section.

1.8   THE APPROACH IN OUTLINE

The process of deriving a model of the business which is described in this text consists of a number of phases, most of which are shown in Fig. 1.13. Further elements of the methodology are shown in Fig. 1.14, which also shows the chapter numbers for the corresponding parts of the methodology.

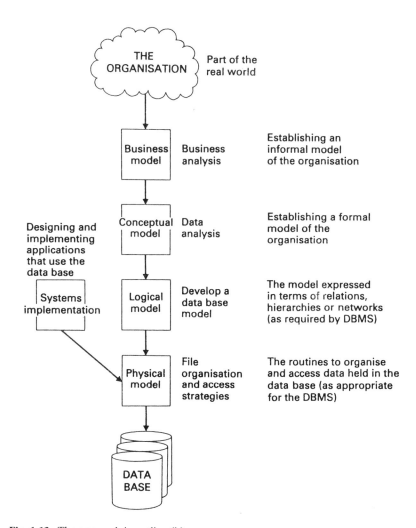

Fig. 1.13. The approach in outline (b).

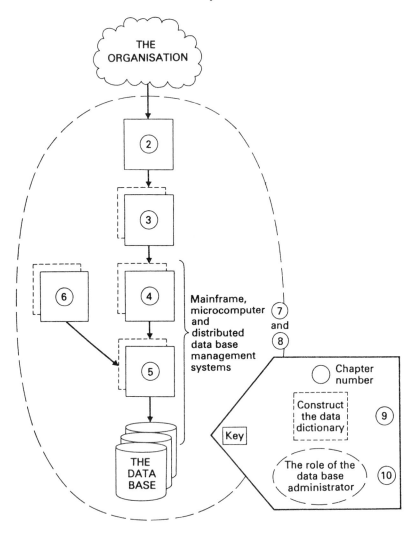

Fig. 1.14. The approach in outline (c).

The first phase of the methodology consists of an overview of the organisation. The analysts require to know the organisational structure, including an outline description of the roles of management personnel. This will guide the analysts in determining who to interview, when to interview them, and what questions to ask. It is necessary to find out what are the goals of the firm. This will be helpful because it will then be possible to discover the types of information required for management to make better decisions. There are a number of diagrammatic aids which can be used at this time. These are described in chapter 2. Another important feature of the **business analysis** phase is a political one. It is possible to discover which strategies for informations systems implementation will be acceptable to the organisation and how best to approach the human problems associated with change. These are likely to be more difficult to solve than the technical problems. Business analysis, therefore, lays the foundation for the work that follows.

Once business analysis is complete, it is possible to derive a formal model of the organisation, referred to as the **conceptual model** (sometimes called the **infological model**). At this stage the analyst identifies the various facts about the organisation and then analyses this data. The facts can be represented as objects of interest, called entities, and data about these objects of interest, called attributes. In my university department, courses, students, and lecturers, could be described as entities. The course entity will have attributes such as course name, description, level, and duration. The analyst will also be interested in relationships between entities. Thus students are likely to be taught by many lecturers. The model so formed is a formal representation of the organisation, showing the data and the data structures. The processes involved in deriving the conceptual model are collectively known as data analysis. The analysts will use interviewing, observation and other methods to obtain the information required. There are a number of documentation tools available, such as entity-relationship diagrams. These are useful aids to communication, help to ensure that the work is carried out in a thorough manner, and ease the mapping processes that follow data analysis. Entities can be represented as relations (see Fig. 1.11) and chapter 3 also looks at relational theory.

Having derived the conceptual model, it is possible to map this model onto a computer Data Base Management System (DBMS). This **logical model** can take a number of forms, depending on the DBMS. In some DBMS, as we see in chapter 4, the data model transferred to the system is defined in terms of relations. Other DBMS view the data relationships in terms of tree structures, known as hierarchies. A simple hierarchy is shown as Fig. 1.15. Here, a manager of a department in a business has two subordinates, of assistant manager status, and each of these have subordinate clerks. Network DBMS will support the representation of rather more complex relationships called networks. These many-to-many relationships are best illustrated in the example shown as Fig. 1.16 which represents a firm which receives parts from a number of suppliers. One supplier may supply a number of parts (for example,

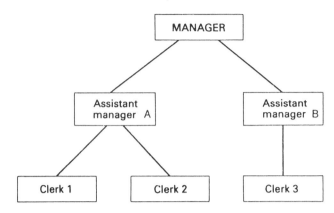

Fig. 1.15. A hierarchical data structure.

SUPPLIER NAME	SUPPLIER ADDRESS	SUPPLIER NUMBER		PART NUMBER	DESCRIPTION
		1		A	
		2		B	
		3		C	
		4		D	

Fig. 1.16. A network data structure.

supplier 1 supplies part A and part B). Conversely, one part can be supplied by a number of suppliers (part B is supplied by suppliers 1, 2, and 3).

The next phase concerns the mapping of the data structures presented to the DBMS, usually in the form of relations, hierarchies or networks, onto a computer medium. It also has to store the data itself. The way that the data is organised on disk and the way that the data is accessed from disk is known as file organisation and file access respectively. Many DBMS offer a number of ways of file organisation and access, and the choice will depend on efficiency considerations. This **physical model** is discussed in chapter 5. There is a further mapping related to the very technical aspects of computer storage such as the design of backing storage media, but this is considered outside the scope of this text.

Once the data base is created, the subsystems can be designed and implemented using the data base. In *this* chapter we have discussed the limitations of conventional systems analysis. In chapter 6, structured systems analysis and design methods are discussed along with prototyping, participation, and other ways of developing applications. Although the methodology appears to suggest that data analysis and data base creation will be completed for the organisation before systems are implemented, this presents an unrealistic scenario. Management will want an earlier pay-off and it is much more likely that data analysis and data base creation will be carried out on one local area (such as a department) at a time and **systems implemented** which are relevant for that department or division.

Chapter 7 looks at a number of **Data Base Management Systems**. Two bases for comparison have already been discussed: the form of the logical model and the range of file access and organisation methods supported. A very important feature of DBMS is the user interface. Many DBMS offer host language access, that is, the application program will be written in a programming language such as Cobol. Most DBMS will also offer some form of query language which will allow non-computer people to access the data base. There are a number of types of language, including some which are supposed to be similar to natural languages. A query language may be suitable for the 'casual user'. A casual user can be someone who has little or no knowledge of computing, limited experience of using a computer, and has little time to practice skills in computing.

A separate chapter has been included on **microcomputers, distributed data bases** and **data base machines**. The facilities that you can expect on a microcomputer data base will be considerably less than those on a mainframe system. However, data bases on microcomputers are becoming more like their mainframe counterparts, and they do give much more user control. This chapter also considers distributed data bases. Here, the data base is split between a number of sites. The users of the data base can use the data on other sites and may not be aware of the source of the data. Data base machines, that is computer systems devoted to data base use, are not commercially widespread at present, although they are of significant interest.

Chapter 9 looks at **data dictionary systems**. These are software tools for recording and processing information about the data that an organisation processes and uses. Originally these systems were designed merely as documentation tools but they have evolved as an essential feature of the systems environment and are of particular importance to the data base administrator who can use the data dictionary to keep track of the data on the data base and, in general, control its use.

It is essential that the organisation sets firm standards so that data which is shared by many users is not corrupted, privacy requirements are followed, and some users of the data base are not using it to the detriment of others. The role of the **data base administrator** (DBA) is discussed in chapter 10. Although these two chapters come at the end of the text, they are possibly the most important. As seen in Fig. 1.14, the data dictionary is being built up and used in four of the five main phases, and the DBA has an influence on all aspects of the methodology. A **case study** which illustrates the application of the methodology is given as an Appendix.

It must be emphasised that not all aspects of the methodology described in this text will be appropriate for all organisations and all applications systems. Furthermore, for different projects, different aspects take on different emphases. The approach is as flexible as possible within the overall framework.

REFERENCES

Crowe, T. and Avison, D.E. (1980) *Management Information from Data Bases*. Macmillan, London.
> This text discusses many of the subjects of this chapter from a management rather than technological perspective.

Daniels, A. and Yeats, D.A. (1971) *Basic Training in Systems Analysis* (2nd edn). Pitman, London.
> This text covers the conventional approach to systems analysis as proposed by the National Computing Centre in 1971. It describes the methodology and its associated documentation standards.

Date, C.J. (1981) *An Introducion to Database Systems* (3rd edn). Addison-Wesley, London.
> An introduction to data base management. It looks in detail at the three major forms of logical schema and also contains chapters on DBMS packages and query languages.

Gane, C.P. and Sarson, T. (1979) *Structured Systems Analysis: Tools and Techniques*. Prentice-Hall, Englewood Cliffs.
> This book looks at structured systems analysis and design techniques and contains chapters on data dictionaries and the relational model.

Sundgren, B. (1985) *Data Bases and Data Models*. Studentlitteratur, Lund.
> Provides a good, simple explanation of many of the concepts used in this chapter.

Wood-Harper, A.T, Antill, Lyn and Avison, D.E. (1985) *Information Systems Definition: The Multiview Approach.* Blackwell Scientific, Oxford.
This approach emphasises the human and social aspects of information systems development.

Chapter 2

Business Analysis

2.1 INTRODUCTION

Before we can carry out a detailed examination of the organisation in order to produce a data model which will then be implemented on a data base, it is necessary to carry out an overview of the organisation. The analysts need to gain a general appreciation of the business. This background information will include an examination of the goals of the organisation, the company structure and the roles of key personnel. This will help the analyst to construct an interview plan. Following preliminary interviews, the analysts will be able to construct an information model and attempt to find out in outline the information needs of the organisation. This information will also be useful in deciding on the approach to adopt for information systems development.

Some practitioners argue that a very detailed analysis of the organisation should be carried out at this time. The danger here, however, is that analysing the working of the company to such a very detailed level early in the life of the project, might cause the analysts to be 'biased' towards the present methods of processing. One of the main requirements of the analysts is that they view the company in a fresh and open way. But an overall impression of the company is still necessary and one of the most useful ways to gain and to communicate this knowledge is to create an information model. This model shows the main functions and the flows of information in the organisation.

One of the important 'philosophical' bases of this text is **systems theory**. One of the ideas of systems theory is that by breaking complex relationships into subsets, information may be lost. In other words, the whole is greater than the sum of the parts. The inter-relationships between the parts are of crucial significance. The systems approach focuses on the organisation as a whole and is concerned with the performance of the organisation and not on the specific requirements of any one department. For this reason the information model attempts to show the information system at the level of the organisation rather than at the level of a particular process or department. Even so, it is usually difficult to persuade employees to see this organisation-wide perspective. One of the advantages of the data base approach is that it permits the sharing of data between departments. The data base is viewed as a resource of the organisation. In conventional data processing, on the other hand, files are seen as a department or single application resource. Conventional files are not usually shared between applications.

The terms **information** and **data** represent different things, and a data model and an information model are also different. Data elements represent unstructured facts. A person's date of birth or driving licence number are examples of data. A date of birth (25/7/76) associated with a driving licence number (78700199) and an identity number (19873) could be used to give the *information* that a person whose identity number is 19873 possesses a driving licence, even though he is under the minimum legal age for driving motor vehicles. The information comes from selecting data and presenting it in such a way that it is meaningful to the user. The data base will contain the facts of interest to the company. The information system will transform the data and present these facts accurately, in a way relevant to the appropriate recipient, in the correct level of detail, and when required.

Although data does not appear at first light to be a resource of the organisation, it certainly is a resource, as it is essential for the organisation to operate effectively. If a company 'lost' its accounts data, it would represent a serious loss and one which would be difficult to recover from. Some firms sell data, such as their customers' names and addresses which can be used by other companies for mailing lists. But data is costly to collect, store and keep up-to-date. It is also costly to transform data into information. The information systems will access data from the data base and transform it into information which the organisation can use. The value of information can be readily appreciated. For example, accurate information about future weather conditions will help the manager of a shop to determine whether to buy stocks of ice cream or stocks of soup. Poor information is likely to prove very costly for the shop owner. Information systems can give the information which will assist managers to make better decisions. These decisions may have very long-term consequences and involve huge investments of money.

As can be seen from Fig. 2.1, **information systems** are designed to help managers make better decisions. The model assumes that the manager can specify his information requirements and that these can be predicted by the system. The system then has to transform these requirements for information into requirements for data. The data will be retrieved from the data base, assuming that it has already been collected and stored. Otherwise a data collection exercise is necessary to capture

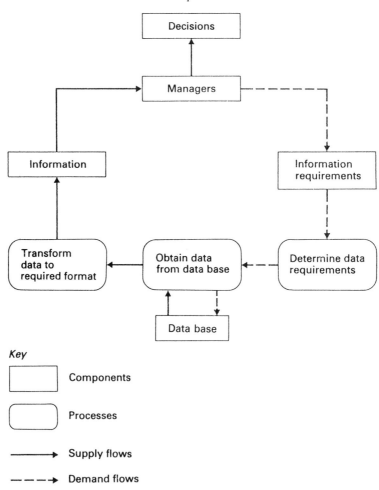

Fig. 2.1. The basic information system.

the data and store it in the data base. Having retrieved the raw data, it needs to be transformed into the required information, perhaps by some preceding analysis work. The information can then be presented to the manager who now has the opportunity to make good or at least better decisions.

The decisions ought to be directed towards achieving the goals of the organisation. These are discussed in the next section. A description of the roles of management (and of the users in general) and the information requirements supporting those roles is given in section 2.3. A framework for information systems can be shown pictorially as an information model, and this is described in section 2.4. This model can be used as a basis for discussions between the analysts and management, as it is a good communication tool. It frequently goes through a series of modifications as a result of the managers' contributions. The strategies for developing information systems are discussed in section 2.6. This is preceded by a section on the people involved in the technological change who will play a major role in deciding what strategy to adopt and in following that strategy through. Just as 'the users' need to be defined, so do 'the analysts'. The final section of this chapter stresses the importance of participation by managers and all users. The more radical strategies will not be feasible unless the political climate is conducive to major change.

2.2 GOALS OF THE ORGANISATION

Theoreticians used to talk of organisations having just one goal, frequently profit maximisation. According to this view, the organisation was 'tuned' to maximise this one goal. The truth is that businesses have a number of goals. These could include increasing the size of their market, long term survival, the welfare of their employees and improving their public image. Obviously most firms would readily sacrifice some profit if it meant that they were likely to be in business for some time. It could be that there are major goals which businesses fulfil, such as maximising the return on capital, whilst having shorter term aims, such as increasing turnover. During recent times, the main goal of many firms may have been long term survival.

The goals of different types of organisation will vary greatly. The goal of a health authority may be to promote the health and hygiene of the people in its catchment area. Those of a church, hospital, business or charity are likely to be very different. Some goals may conflict. In a retail organisation there may be one goal, to increase sales targets, which may conflict with others, such as to reduce staff levels or increase profit margins. If sales levels do increase, it may be as a result of increasing sales staff or decreasing profit margins.

This type of information may well be gleaned from interviewing members of the directorate. Another source of information is the company review and accounts which are usually published annually as part of the statement to the shareholders or governors. This may also help in providing an outline of the structure of the organisation: its divisions and management hierarchy. All this company background can help the analysts get a 'feel' for the organisation, particularly if they are from outside the company. Information systems work is frequently carried out by external consultants or people recently recruited from outside, because they have had experience of such work elsewhere.

It is also useful to look at the environment of the organisation, because the actions of customers, suppliers, trade unions, competitors and the government can have far-reaching effects on the business. Management must observe and react to changes in economic and social factors. Although it is not always possible to record all this information in the modelling process, it is necessary to be at least aware of these factors. Figure 2.2 paints a sketch of the business universe having six major subsystems and a number of environmental systems which relate to the business.

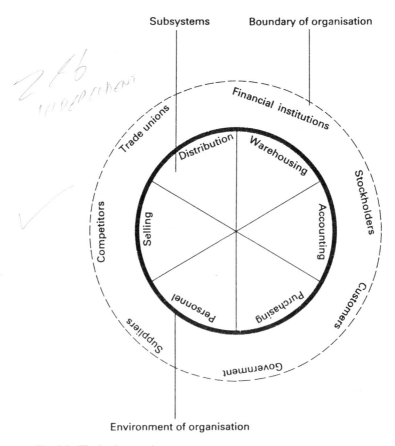

Fig. 2.2. The business universe.

2.3 COMPANY STRUCTURE AND ROLES OF KEY PERSONNEL

Before the development team of analysts engrosses itself into data analysis, which is partly carried out through interview and observation, it is necessary to consider the structure of the organisation and the roles played by members of the management team. Without this knowledge, it is not possible to decide on the people to interview, in which order they should be interviewed, and the level and subject matter of the questions to ask.

Most organisations can be looked upon as having three layers of management. At the top layer are the board of directors. They are responsible for the long range planning activities of the firm and they will set the overall goals. Middle management, typically heads of departments, will ensure that these policies are carried out and will act upon exceptional conditions. The operations level will be responsible for the day to day operations of the organisation. These will include the chief clerks and foremen who control the daily ordering, production and distribution processes.

It is important to identify these people in the early stages of the project. In a retail company having a number of department stores and warehouses in the country, strategic management will include the directors of finance, trading, personnel, and buying. Middle management will include the heads of the branches, branch accountants, and warehouse managers. Operations management will include department managers, warehouse foremen, and the head clerks. This structure is shown in Fig.2.3.

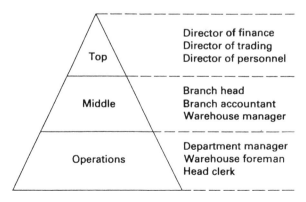

Fig. 2.3. Layers of management for a retail company.

Top management is clearly very important to the organisation, and managers are realising that management information systems can help them make better decisions. Although the euphoria associated with automatic decision-making has largely gone, the more realistic concept of **decision-support systems** has certainly not disappeared. Management need these systems in order to help them establish sustainable goals and to provide information relating to the long-term decisions of the organisation. Examples of the types of decisions that managers will make could include where to site new factories, whether to merge with other companies, or whether to drop a product range. Information to help top management make these decisions could be provided by the system. When the model of the organisation is implemented on a data base, it

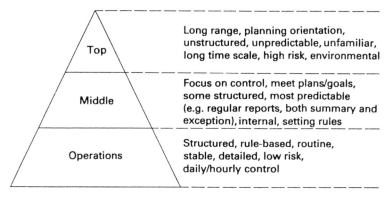

Fig. 2.4. Types of decisions made by management.

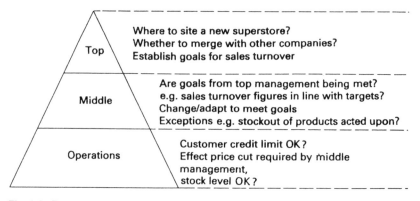

Fig. 2.5. Examples of decisions in a retail company.

will be possible for managers to make enquiries of the data base. The types of information required will tend to be unpredictable and unstructured so that data base access will need to be flexible. Such enquiries may be answered by getting data from a number of different areas in the data base, a requirement sometimes referred to as 'navigating' through the data base. Sometimes the information system will be used to simulate the effects of actions of managers.

For all three layers of the management hierarchy, the types of decision, examples of the decisions, and the types of information required to support this decision-making are shown in Figs 2.4, 2.5 and 2.6 respectively. As well as determining the information needed now and in the near future, some regard must be given to the difficult task of trying to foresee information needs in the future. Priorities are also required to be assigned to information needs, and these priorities have to be assigned by management.

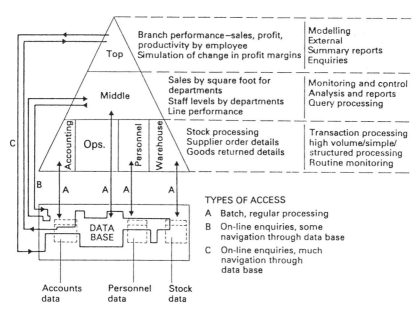

Fig. 2.6. Information required by managers of retail company.

Middle management will ensure that the goals set by top management are being met. Reports about performance will be produced regularly so that the results can be compared to the target, and the facilities of the data base will also be made available to managers using a query language. The unusual, for example products which are unavailable from stock, may also be reported on, so that managers may act on these exceptional conditions. This will allow **management by exception**. Much of the information required here will be predictable and internal. For example, each week the manager might want a list of those customers who have not cleared their debts. Decisions at the operations management level can frequently be made automatically. These decisions tend to be structured, rule-based and routine. For example, a computer system can check stock levels and produce a supplier's order request in good time to ensure that there is always supplies of products in stock.

It is important that the information given by the system is **relevant** to the particular recipient and therefore in the correct level of detail. This could be in summary form — **management by summary**. It must also be **accurate**, or at least accurate enough for the recipient, and **timely**, as information provided too late for the particular purpose is useless (and hence not 'information' at all). The system should also be **adaptable** so that it can respond to the changing needs of the user. This means that the data analysis stage is as crucial as the computer systems implementation stage. The most sophisticated technology is useless if the data is not appropriate; and the most accurate data collection exercise is useless if the technology does not support timely and adaptable systems.

The information requirements of some personnel may be inferred from their job description. It may be easy to find out formal descriptions of the **roles** of personnel. Many firms publish full job descriptions along with details of the reporting structure. Equally important is the **informal structure**. Important parts of the job could be carried out at break times or through telephone calls. Official communication channels may be side-stepped. The analysts therefore need a 'feel' for the informal as well as the formal system.

This exercise will also reveal the likely users of the information system. One fact will be immediately obvious: the users of the information system will not all be trained computer experts. Untrained computer users may make particular requests of the system or they might 'browse' through files. This type of casual usage is likely to grow. Therefore, although some access to the data base will be made by **professional users** through computer programs written in Cobol and other programming languages, some, perhaps most, access will be made by untrained users. Some of these users will be **regular users**, that is they may make daily or weekly access to particular parts of the system and they may be willing to train in the use of particular facilities. Clerical staff who may be required to input data into the system will be expected to train in the use of the system. Some users will be **casual users**, and these users, frequently middle or top managers, will have had little experience of computing. Their use of the system will be varied. Each day's enquiries could be different and based on different parts of the data base. It is therefore difficult to train such staff, even if they had the time and inclination to practice the skills necessary. For this reason, there must be query languages available which make it easy for managers to use the system.

2.4   THE INFORMATION MODEL

Having an overall view of the nature of the business, the people in it, and its information needs, it is possible to construct an information model. This is largely a pictorial representation of the organisation in outline and it can be used as a basis for discussions with management. As a result of these discussions, the information model may well change in content.

It will show the major applications systems of the organisation and the flows of resources between them. It is particularly useful in providing some **boundaries** and **interfaces** to the organisation. Some logical files have also been included in the model. These give the analyst ideas on what sort of data will be needed to support information systems. But all this information is in outline. It is NOT intended to suggest processes and detailed data storage facilities.

Figure 2.7 shows one iteration in the creation of an information model for a retail business. The final version will be developed after several interviews with management personnel. I have included in the model some of the names of the smaller subsystems, sometimes referred to as modules, in each of the larger systems areas. These include stock control, supplier accounting, customer accounting, and personnel. Within stock control, for example, are supplier ordering, warehouse management and quality control. The four major subsystems are carried out at different locations, by different personnel, and therefore formed 'natural' boundaries. By the time the model has been constructed, the analyst has gained an appreciation of the business in outline. With this knowledge it will be possible to agree an appropriate 'strategy' for the systems project. This will be a decision of the systems planning team whose function will also be to oversee the development of the information systems project.

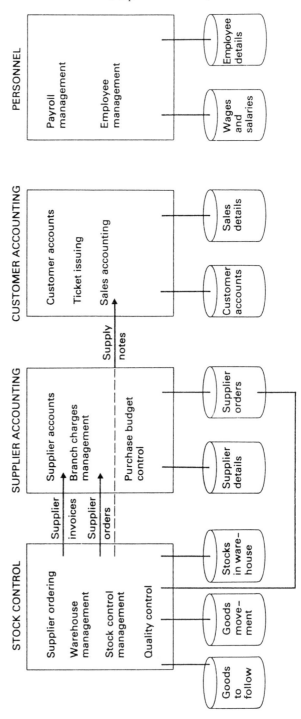

Fig. 2.7. Developing the information model for a retail company.

2.5   THE SYSTEMS PLANNING TEAM

The systems planning team's main function is to coordinate and control the information systems project. It is important that the team is not dominated by the technologists, although it will certainly include them. Corporate experience, rather than technical expertise, should dominate. The information systems project will affect the whole organisation and therefore it is necessary to include top management in the team. This would suggest that the chairman of the systems planning team could typically be one of the company directors, who would carry the status suggested. Other management representatives of the systems planning team could include the production manager, marketing manager and other department heads. Such a high-powered team should ensure that the project carries the prestige necessary to carry its proposals through the organisation. It should also help to get the management commitment behind the project and this will significantly increase the likelihood of its success. Top management will be seen to lead by example.

The information systems project will cause changes to the roles of employees and in working relationships. The systems planning team ought to anticipate problems that may occur. It is therefore necessary to include the personnel manager and a trade union representative in the systems planning team. As we shall see in section 2.7, it is important to keep employees fully informed of the project. Many systems may be excellent from a technological point of view, but fail because of a lack of consideration given to these issues. The new system may be seen as a threat to status and job. Frequently staff will resist the change in ways which may be less dramatic than sabotage, but be equally effective. Once the trust of the workforce has been lost, it is difficult to regain it, even if future change is perceived to be in the interest of employees.

The two most important representatives from the innovating group will be the data base administrator and the chief analyst who is likely to be the project leader. In some circumstances the data base administrator will be the project leader. The need for a data base administrator is clearly recognised in the methodology, although the role is often filled late in the life of the project, perhaps when it is too late. The data base administrator can help the systems planning team decide on standards for communication, documentation, project development and evaluation, and help to implement these standards.

Frequently the systems planning team also includes an outside consultant. This person will not have a background in the organisation, and a perceived lack of departmental bias will be useful when arbitrating on differences of opinion. Another reason for 'outsiders' expertise could be the lack of internal expertise in projects of this kind. Figure 2.8 shows the possible membership of the systems planning team.

Fig. 2.8. The systems planning team.

One of the most important tasks of the systems planning team is to determine the boundaries of the information system. The decision may be implicit by the membership of the team, even so, the boundaries must be defined explicitly. For a corporation like Unilever, which has a number of companies in its overall control, the boundary may be defined to include one or a number of these companies. With some organisations, the various subsystems may be so large that the boundary might be defined around accounts or personnel. This may be particularly appropriate where subsystems do not naturally relate, that is, there is little data travelling between them or where one or two areas, such as production and invoicing in the case of the electricity supply industry, dominate the business.

Once the overall information system's boundary has been fixed, it will be itself divided into lower-level systems (sometimes known as subsystems) for separate development. These arrangements will largely depend on the strategy adopted for the development of information systems. The determination of this strategy, a positive plan for the development of information systems, is a particularly important role of the systems planning team and is discussed separately in the next section. The data analyst has to know the boundary of the data analysis exercise and how much time to devote to it. The systems planning team will ensure that the subsystems are developed according to the plan which allows for some form of integration later. Each subsystem should be seen as a natural subsytem of the larger system. The priority for developing these subsystems will depend on **potential benefit, urgency of**

need, probability of success or **natural precedence**, which could be described as the next 'piece of the jigsaw'.

The systems planning team will overview the development of the project, although they will appoint a **systems development team** to control its day-to-day running. The constituents of the systems development team will depend on the degree of participation adopted, although it is certainly usual, if *not* always desirable, that it is biased towards the technologists. The systems development team will include the chief analyst and the data base administrator who are both likely to be members of the systems planning team. The project leader, who will be one of these two representatives, is likely to act as chairman of the development team. Other likely members of the systems development team will be data analysts who will be involved in developing the data model, and systems analysts, systems designers and programmers who will specify the needs of the users, and design and develop the various subsystems and programs (or choose and modify the application packages). The final constituents of the systems development team will be the representatives from the user departments. These are likely to include the department managers and possibly people who will use the system when it is implemented. User involvement is discussed in section 2.7 and further in section 6.3.

2.6 STRATEGY FOR INFORMATION SYSTEMS DEVELOPMENT

There are a number of alternative strategies that the systems planning team may decide to adopt. It is essential that full consideration is given to the evaluation of which strategy or combination of strategies is appropriate for the organisation, because inadequate planning will lead to failure — however good the tools and techniques used in the data base project. The particular strategy appropriate to the organisation will depend to a large extent on the political and financial circumstances of the organisation. Attempts in the past to implement change may have left scars, and the spirit of trust, confidence and cooperation necessary to implement radical change will be difficult to achieve. The organisation may not be used to changes: both with regard to the roles of personnel and the technology used.

Following Blumenthal (1969), six strategies are discussed, although the meaning of each has been changed somewhat to take account of the technological and other developments that have taken place since that text was published. These strategies should not be considered as mutually exclusive: usually the systems planning team decides that the best strategy for their organisation is one which is a combination of those discussed, and I have attempted to incorporate some of these possibilities.

One strategy for implementing information systems would proceed by breaking up the information systems project according to the departmental structure of the organisation. This **Organisation Chart approach** would be carried out by implementing each department's system in turn. In the retail organisation looked at in this chapter, this could start at the sales office, then to accounting, warehousing, production, buying, and personnel. This has the particular advantage of avoiding possible political problems that may have occurred if a more radical strategy had been adopted, because the workplace and working relationships will probably remain intact, although the roles of the employees in it may change. The management team is also likely to remain the same.

For the overall systems project to be successful, however, the design needs to allow for **Integration Later**. An opportunity will be lost if systems in the various departments cannot 'talk' to each other and share the same data base. Thought has to be given to future integration at the initial design stage, otherwise subsequent integration will be very difficult and expensive. There will be no 'common language' between the systems. The systems planning team has a particularly important role to ensure a 'design for integration' and also to prevent any delay in this integration. The longer the delay, the more difficult integration becomes.

With many organisations, following the departmental boundaries of the firm will not be a good strategy. Many processes, such as sales order processing, will cross departmental boundaries. The sales order may first enter the sales office, then be processed by the warehouse, then the production department, then distribution, and finally the accounts department. This reflects the following processes. The order is received by the sales office; checks are made in the warehouse to see if the sub-assemblies are in stock; a schedule is made in the production department and the products manufactured; the goods are despatched by the distribution department; and the invoice typed up in accounts and sent to the customer. It is not surprising therefore that the strategy for information systems development which follows the existing departmental structure of the firm may be the easiest politically, but not the one that gains the most from the data base and informations systems project. Even conventional processing is inter-departmental.

An alternative approach would break up the organisation according to some other criteria but implement each section in turn and allow for integration later. Again, without this design for integration it will be very difficult to achieve the expected gains of data bases and information systems. This alternative design may be based on management needs, a sort of **Top Down approach**. This approach can be a good strategy where the information required by top management is fairly stable in terms of content, level of detail, and frequency. Designing the information systems project around management needs may, however, ignore the operational requirements. To fulfil operational requirements as well may lead to data being collected, validated and stored more than once. However, there are circumstances where management information cannot be derived from operational data.

In following the above approaches, there may be a tendency to design in terms of applications which mirror the present requirements of the business. There is a danger that these needs will change. The importance of developing the data base without regard to applications has already been stressed. Applications requirements frequently change: data is more stable. **The Data Collection approach** stresses the importance of data collection and analysis without regard to functions. The data is collected for an area of the organisation. It is then classified and the relationships between the data elements are recorded for use when required. One of the criticisms of this approach is that data may be collected which is never used subsequently. However, there is a two stage process: data modelling *and* mapping to the data base. Data which is unlikely to be used need not be transferred to the data base.

The Data Base approach need not necessarily be associated with data collection and classification. Data analysis can be useful without data bases. The process of modelling the organisation should result in a better understanding of the business. The data and data structures that have been identified can be mapped on to conventional computer files or clerical files and not necessarily data bases. Similarly, the data base can be built up piecemeal without an organised data analysis exercise. However, the resulting data base system may well not prove as flexible nor as long-lasting as one formed by a preceding data analysis.

This text therefore proposes that data analysis is followed by data base implementation. The drawback associated with this approach is that data may be held indefinitely with no use being made of it. It is an important role of the data base administrator to control attempts to keep data on the data base indefinitely and to ensure that data entering the data base is likely to be of use in the near future. The functions of the organisation should therefore be kept in mind in data analysis, even though 'in theory' data analysis attempts to look at the organisation independently of the processes.

Implicit in the discussion of this data analysis and data base approach is that a **Total System** is implemented. By this is meant that design, development and implementation will be for the organisation as a whole. The organisation is regarded as a 'green field', able and willing both to accept and adapt to a completely changed information systems environment. However, rarely can the political, social, and other forces existing in the organisation countenance such change. Such an approach also assumes that management would be willing to pay for a large project, accept the risks involved and get little reward in terms of information systems for a number of years. Obviously this is not a realistic assumption. The systems planning team will have to ensure that rewards come during and not only after the full information systems project is implemented. The project must therefore be divided into chunks, and data analysis, data base and information systems implemented in each of these divisions in turn. Whilst doing so, the systems planning team must not lose sight of the overall plan.

2.7 MANAGEMENT AND USER INVOLVEMENT

The previous section has brought to light the difficulties of carrying out a radical approach to the development of information systems in many organisations. The reasons for failure in these projects tend not to lie in the technical side, though the technology is complex, nor in the economic side, though the cost of these systems is very high: the reasons for failure are more likely to be due to **people problems**, which may show themselves by the lack of cooperation when the system is being developed and a resistance to the changes that occur when the systems are implemented.

People may regard the change negatively. They may think that their jobs will be less secure, that they might lose the independence that they previously enjoyed, that their relationships with others will change for the worse, and that their work will change. Some of these can be positive changes for the staff, but they may be perceived as negative.

Unless steps have been taken to ensure that the people of the organisation are fully informed of the changes that are proposed, that they support the changes, and see themselves as gaining from them, then there is no reason to assume that they will cooperate with the changes: indeed, there is good reason to assume that they will try to ensure that the changes do not work. Their experience of the ways in which change has been effected in the past will also contribute to their present reactions. If the trust and confidence has been ruptured previously, it will be difficult to regain. The management climate within the organisation and the way in which grievances are heard and fears discussed are important. **Organisational Learning**, where the 'organisation' stores experiences in forms, procedures and rules, and uses it to teach new staff and retrain others, can encourage adaptiveness to change. Such practices need to be established so that change becomes the norm, is expected, and is viewed positively.

Such inducements as salary, status and job interest, could also be used to ensure that staff might enjoy their new roles. The work force should be informed of the likely changes in good time. Rumours about impending changes will occur anyway, and staff not fully informed are likely to fear the worst. Those that can get jobs will leave, and these are likely to be the staff that the organisation wants to keep most. Further, resistance can be caused by fears which are not based on fact. Education, about what computers can and cannot do, will be more important than training in the early stages of the project.

It is important to communicate to the user not only the potential advantages of the information systems approach, of relevant, timely, accurate, understandable, and up-to-date, information which is provided to the correct level of detail, highlighting critical factors which control the firm's success, but of potential pitfalls that should be avoided. More information is not necessarily better: it may be too detailed for 'digestion' or irrelevant to the particular decision-maker. Decision-making will not necessarily improve just because the information is available: it may be ignored as many managers will prefer to keep to the combination of intuition, experience and judgement to make decisions. There should be wide discussion within the organisation of these aspects so that management is aware of the pitfalls.

The data base project is very expensive and difficult to justify in tangible terms. The major product is information, not tangible objects like stocks of goods which are easier to evaluate. What is the value of information? There are obvious advantages of the information which could include better costing, better cash flow, improved customer relations, and it should lead to better decisions being made by management, but it is difficult to put a monetary value on this. Yet it is important to convince management of these gains, otherwise it will be extremely unlikely that the information systems projects will be given the go-ahead, and even if this is achieved, they are unlikely to be successful.

It is also important that top management are 'seen' to support the system, are committed to it and that they participate in the change. They *should* benefit most from the system, as they are the information requirers. This commitment will encourage others to fall in with the change. A general air of good communications and user participation will also help. These users will include the clerical workers who will be concerned with the input of data to the system and the verification of its output. It is very important that user groups do contribute to the change and that their suggestions are not merely dealt with by paying lip service. Again, user involvement should help to lessen the likelihood of a general level of mistrust and a lack of confidence.

Business analysis, therefore should be looked upon as a two-way exercise — an opportunity to inform, help and convince, as much as an opportunity to find out about the organisation. It is therefore an important part of the methodology. It has helped in identifying the concerns of the business, its goals and its information requirements. It has identified the people concerned with information systems development. It has also helped in looking at the functions of the business in outline. This is enough to help the systems planning team draw limits to the data modelling exercise. It has set a strategy for the next stages in the development of the information systems and data base project and, through the encouragement of user involvement and management participation, a 'style' likely to lead to its successful completion.

REFERENCES

Ackoff, R.L. (1967) 'Management Misinformation Systems', *Management Science*, **14**, B147–56.
  An interesting discussion on the pitfalls of Management Information Systems.
Blumenthal, S.C. (1969) *Management Information Systems: A Framework for Planning and Control.* Prentice-Hall, Englewood-Cliffs.
  This text covers the analysis of organisations for the development of information systems.
Crowe, T. and Avison, D.E. (1980) *Management Information from Data Bases.* Macmillan, London.
Cyert, R.M. and March, J.G. (1963) *A Behavioral Theory of the Firm.* Prentice-Hall, Englewood Cliffs.
  This text contains a discussion on the goals of the firm.
Davis, G.B. and Olsen, M.H. (1985) *Management Information Systems: Conceptual Foundations, Structure, and Development* (2nd edn). McGraw-Hill, New York.
  This text provides an excellent grounding on information systems.

Chapter 3

The Conceptual Schema:
Data Analysis and the Relational Model

3.1 INTRODUCTION

Conventional systems analysis procedures were applied to single applications that were the first to be computerised in the organisation. When applications being developed are an integrated part of a total system, these techniques of analysis prove inadequate. The most obvious situation which requires a different approach is the development of a data base. In a data base environment, many applications share the same data. The data base is looked upon as a common asset.

Data analysis techniques were largely developed to cater for the implementation of data base systems, although that does not mean that they cannot be applied to non-data base situations, such as the development of applications on a microcomputer. Data analysis can also be of interest to management as a way of viewing their organisation.

The methodology represents a significant change in the development of computing systems away from the technology, in particular, hardware and software (including programming techniques and algorithms), and towards data and the way it is structured. The emphasis on programming in earlier systems was natural: firstly because computers demanded greater programming skill, and secondly because the professional was interested in the possibility of solving complex programming problems using the basic instruction set of the computer.

The emphasis has now moved to data because, if it can be made available in the correct form, programming applications present much less of a problem. Data is a very important resource of the business. The algorithms required for normal data processing are relatively simple. As computer systems become more powerful, less stress needs to be paid to problems of implementation (availability of storage, for example) and more to problems independent of implementation.

One of the most important techniques of data analysis described in the text is entity modelling. Just as an accountant might use a financial model, the analyst can develop an entity model. The entity model is just another view of the organisation, but it is a particular perception of reality and it can be used to solve a number of problems. The model produced provides an excellent and novel way of viewing the business. Systems analysis in general, and data analysis is a branch of systems analysis, is an art, not an exact science. There can be a number of ways to derive a reasonable model and there are a number of reasonable models (there are of course an infinite number of wrong models).

Good models will be a fair representation of the 'real world'. The entity model can be looked on as a discussion document and its coincidence with the real world is verified in discussions with the various users. However, the analyst should be aware that variances between the model and a particular user's view could be due to the narrow perception of that user. The model should be a global view. The size of that 'globe' — a department, a number of departments, a company or an organisation — having been agreed in the business analysis phase (section 2.6).

An **entity-relationship** model views the organisation as a set of data elements, known as entities, which are the things of interest to the organisation, and relationships between these entities. This model enables the computer specialist to design appropriate computer systems for the organisation, but it also provides management with a unique tool for perceiving the business process. The essence of rational scientific problem solving is to be able to perceive the complex, 'messy', real world in such a manner that the solution to any problem may be easier. This model is 'simple' in that it is fairly easy to understand and to use.

Each entity can be represented diagrammatically by **soft boxes** (rectangles with rounded corners). Relationships between the entities are shown by lines between the soft boxes. A first approach to an entity model for the Department of Computer Science at Aston is given in Fig. 3.1. The reader will soon detect a number of important things of interest that have been omitted. As the analysts find out more about the organisation, entities will be added to the model.

A mistake frequently made at this stage is to define the entities to reflect the processes of the business, such as stock control, credit control or sales order processing. This could be a valid model of the business but it is not an entity model and cannot be used to produce the flexible data base for the organisation that we require. A data base so created would be satisfactory for some specific applications, but would not be adequate for many applications. Where data analysis differs from conventional systems analysis is that it separates the data structures from the applications which use them. The objective of data analysis is to produce a flexible model which can be easily adapted as the requirements of the users change. Although the applications will need to be changed, this

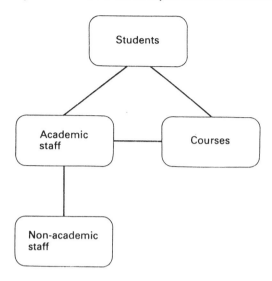

Fig. 3.1. Entity modelling — a first approach.

will not necessarily be true of the data.

The entity-relationship model is a data model, referred to as the **conceptual schema**. The model reflects data in the business, not processes. It is concerned with the data that exists, not how it is used. The entities are quantifiable and can be represented as special tables, known as relations. These were introduced in section 1.4 and typical relations are seen in Fig. 1.11.

The data items (attributes) associated with each entity (or relation) can then be normalised. Normalisation is a set of rules applied to the relations which simplifies the model. These relations can then be mapped onto a data base. The relational model and normalisation are explained in detail in sections 3.6 and 3.7.

3.2 ENTITY-RELATIONSHIP APPROACH

Probably the most widespread technique of data analysis is that proposed by Chen (1976). The major advances described in Chen's paper were helped by the preceding work of the Codasyl Committee (see section 4.4) and Codd (1970). The information algebra proposed in the Codasyl report contained two important concepts: that of an entity as a thing that has reality, and that of joining records on equal values of keys. For modelling reality, it is essential to distinguish between different objects in the real world and understand how they are related to each other. The problem with the original Codasyl proposals is that there is no clear distinction made between the conceptual or user view and the physical or computer view. This distinction is most important because of the inherent flexibility that results from it. Codd's relational model, on the other hand, is not dependent on any specific physical implementation, it is **data independent**.

In Chen's entity-relationship (E-R) model, the real world information is represented by entities and by relationships between entities. The entities, which could include jobs, customers, departments, and suppliers in a typical business, are classified into entity sets. These represent entities and relationships having similar properties. The analyst identifies the entities and relationships before being immersed in the detail, in particular the work of identifying the attributes which define the properties of entities.

Figure 3.2 represents an entity set relating to part of a hospital. The entities described are DOCTORS, PATIENTS and CLINICAL-SESSIONS. The relationships between the entities are also described. That between DOCTORS and PATIENTS and between DOCTORS and CLINICAL-SESSIONS are one-to-many relationships. In other words, DOCTORS can have many PATIENTS, but a PATIENT is only assigned one DOCTOR. Further, DOCTORS can be responsible for many CLINICAL-SESSIONS, but a CLINICAL-SESSION is the responsibility of only one DOCTOR. The other relationship is many-to-many. In other words, a PATIENT can attend a number of CLINICAL-SESSIONS and one CLINICAL-SESSION can be attended by a number of PATIENTS.

The diagram (3.2a) also shows a few attributes of the entities. The particular attribute or group of attributes that uniquely identify an entity occurrence is known as the key attribute or attributes. The 'employee number' is the key attribute of the entity called DOCTOR. Two diagrammatic conventions, both of which are used in business, are shown in Fig. 3.2. The former (Fig. 3.2a) has been adopted in the main body of the text and the latter (Fig. 3.2b) is used in the Appendix for comparative purposes. The first (crow's foot convention) is more widely used, but the second, used for example by Howe (1983), allows the display of uncommitted relationships. These are relationships which have not been defined at this stage. A line between entities without any crow's feet in the first convention would indicate a one-to-one relationship, not an uncommitted relationship.

The technique attempts to separate the data structure from the

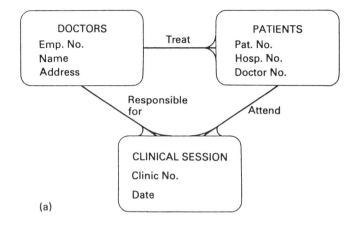

(a)

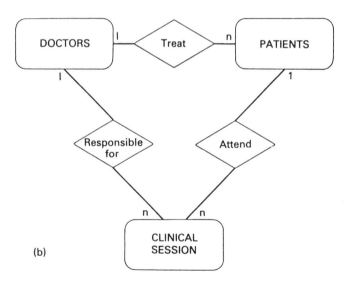

(b)

Fig. 3.2. Two ways of representing an entity set relating to part of a hospital.

functions for which the data may be used. This separation is a useful distinction, although it is often difficult to make in practice. In any case, it is sometimes useful to bear in mind the functions of the data analysed. DOCTORS and PATIENTS are both people, but it is their role, that is what they *do*, that separates the entities. The distinction, formed because of a knowledge of functions, is a useful one to make. However, too much regard to functions will produce a model biased towards particular applications or users.

Another practical problem is that 'global' (organisation-wide) data analysis may be so costly and time-consuming that it is often preferable to carry out entity analysis at a 'local' level, such as the marketing area. If a local entity analysis is carried out, the model can be mapped onto a data base and applications applied to it before another local data analysis is started. This is far more likely to gain management approval because managers can see the expensive exercise paying dividends in a reasonable time scale. An important preliminary step is therefore to define the area for analysis and break this up into distinct sub-areas which can be implemented on a data base and merged later. Local data analysis should also be carried out in phases. The first phase is an overview which leads to the identification of the major things of interest in that area. At the end of the overview phase, it is possible to draw up a second interview plan and the next, longer, phase aims to fill in the detail.

Although it is relatively easy to illustrate the process of modelling in a book or at a lecture, in real life there are problems in deciding how far one should go and what level of detail is appropriate. The level of detail must serve two purposes:

(1) It must be capable of explaining that part of the organisation defined for these purposes by business analysis, and

(2) It must be capable of being translated into the physical model.

It is important to realise that there is no logical or natural point at which the level of detail stops. This is a pragmatic decision. Certainly design teams can put too much effort into the development of the model. Some of the levels of detail that are capable of expression using the methodology outlined are perhaps best left to implementation. An example of this could be entity occurrences of persons who are female, where they relate to (a) patients in a hospital, (b) students at university, and (c) readers in a library. In the patient example, the fact that the person occurrence is female is important, so important that the patient entity may be split into two separate entities — male patients and female patients. In the student example, the fact that the person is female may not be of great significance and therefore there could be an attribute 'sex' of the person entity. In the reader example, the fact that the person is female may be of such insignificance that it is not even included as an attribute. There is a danger here, however, as the analyst must ensure that it will not be significant in any application in the library. This type of debate can only be resolved when looking at the functions in some detail.

3.3 SOME DEFINITIONS

An **entity** is a thing of interest, in other words it is almost anything that you want to define as such. It could include all the resources of the business and it can be extended to cover such things as ORDERS, INVOICES, and PROFIT-CENTRES. It covers concepts as well as objects. It is not data itself, but something about which data should be kept. It is something that can have an independent existence. In creating an entity model, the aim should be to define entities that enable one to describe the business. Such entities as STOCK, ORDERS and CUS-TOMERS are appropriate because they are quantifiable, whereas 'stock control', 'order processing' and 'credit control' are not appropriate because they are functions: what the organisation does, and not things of interest which participate in functions. *Entities will normally be displayed in capitals in this text.* Entities can also be quantified — it is reasonable to ask "how many customers?" or "how many orders per day?", but not "how many credit controls?" An **entity occurrence** is a particular example of an entity which can be uniquely identified. For example 'John Smith & Son' could be an occurrence of the entity CUSTOMER.

An **attribute** is a descriptive value associated with an entity. It is a property of an entity. At a certain stage in the analysis it becomes necessary not only to define each entity but also to record the relevant attributes for each entity. A CUSTOMER entity may be defined and it will have a number of attributes associated with it, such as 'number', 'name', 'address', and so on. *Attributes will normally be displayed in inverted commas in the text.* The values of a set of attributes will distinguish one entity occurrence from another. Attributes are frequent-ly identified during data analysis when entities are being identified, but most come later, particularly in detailed interviews with staff. Many are discovered when checking the entity model with users. An entity may be uniquely identified by one or more of its attributes, the **key attribute(s)**. A 'customer number' may identify an occurrence of the entity CUS-TOMER. A 'customer number' and a 'product number' may together form the key of entity ORDER.

There often arises the problem of distinguishing between an entity and an attribute. In many cases, things that can be defined as entities could also be defined as attributes, and vice versa. We have discussed one example relating to the sex of people. The entity should have importance in itself, otherwise it is an attribute. In practice the problem is not as important as it may seem. The analyst can change his model at a later stage, even when mapping the model onto a data base. Entities participate in functions of the organisation and the attributes are those data elements that are required to support the functions. The best rule of thumb is to ask whether the data element has information about it, in other words does it have attributes? Entities and attributes are further distinguished by their role in events (discussed below).

A **relationship** in an entity model normally represents an association between two entities. A SUPPLIER entity has a relationship with the PRODUCT entity through the relationship *supplies*, that is, SUP-PLIERS *supply* PRODUCTS. *Relationships will normally be italicised in the text.* The next stage in the development of an entity model, having defined the entities and 'fleshed' out the entities with attributes, is to associate related entities by relationships and thus put edges into the model. A relationship normally arises because of:

(1) Association, for example 'CUSTOMER *places* ORDERS'

(2) Structure, for example 'ORDERS *consist of* ORDER LINES'

The association between entities has to be meaningful, the relationship normally has an information content — CUSTOMERS *place* ORDERS. The action *place* describes the relationship between CUS-TOMERS and ORDERS. The name given to the relationship also helps to make the model readable.

The **degree of the relationship** could be one-to-one, one-to-many, or many-to-many. A MAN may only have one WIFE at a time, and a WIFE can have only one HUSBAND at a time. This is an example of a one-to-one (1:1) relationship. A MEMBER OF PARLIAMENT can only represent one constituency, and one CONSTITUENCY can have only one MEMBER OF PARLIAMENT. This is another example of a one-to-one relationship. A one-to-one relationship is represented graphically by a line between the two soft boxes. Very often, a one-to-one relationship can be better expressed as a single entity, with one of the entities forming attributes of the more significant entity.

The relationship between an entity CUSTOMER and another entity ORDERS is usually of a degree one-to-many (1:m). Each CUSTOMER can have a number of outstanding ORDERS, but an ORDER can refer to only one CUSTOMER. This is represented diagrammatically by having a line between the soft boxes and a crow's foot at the 'many' end, that is to the ORDERS in this example.

With a many-to-many (m:n) relationship, each entity can be related to one or more occurrences of the partner entity. A CUSTOMER can *order* many PRODUCTS; and one PRODUCT could be *ordered by* a number of CUSTOMERS. This will be represented diagrammatically by a line joining the CUSTOMER and PRODUCT softboxes with a crow's foot at both ends. These examples of relationships are shown in Fig. 3.3.

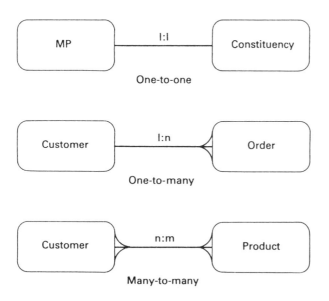

Fig. 3.3. Degrees of a relationship.

Frequently there is useful information associated with many-to-many relationships and it is better to split these into two one-to-many relationships, with a third entity created to link these together. Again, this should only be done if the new entity has some meaning in itself. The relationship between COURSES and LECTURERS is many-to-many, that is, one LECTURER *lectures on* many COURSES and a COURSE is *given by* many LECTURERS. But a new entity, MODULE can be described which may only be *given by* one LECTURER and is part of only one COURSE. Thus a LECTURER *gives* a number of MODULES and a COURSE *consists of* a number of MODULES.

But one MODULE is *given by* only one LECTURER on one COURSE (if this number is the restriction). This is shown in Fig.3.4.

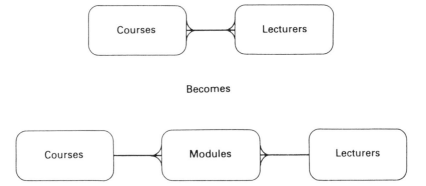

Fig. 3.4. Many-to-many relationships represented as two one-to-many relationships.

Sometimes a 1:m or an m:n relationship is a **fixed degree relationship**. The many-to-many relationship between the entity PARENT and the entity CHILD is 2:n. Some relationships are **optional relationships**. An entity MALE and an entity FEMALE may be joined together by the optional relationship *married to*. There can be more than one relationship between entities. An entity occurrence 'Tom' could be joined with the entity occurrence 'house' by two relationships *owns* and *lives in*. A data structure may also be **involuted** where entity occurrences relate to other occurrences of the same entity. This can be shown diagrammatically by an involuted loop, as in Fig. 3.5. This can occur in the entity EMPLOYEES, where a 'manager' occurrence of the EMPLOYEE entity relates to a 'junior' occurrence of the employee entity by the relationship *manages*.

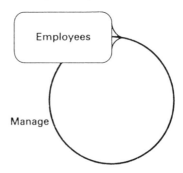

Fig. 3.5. An involuted relationship.

Entities have to support the **Events** that occur in the enterprise. Entities will take part in modelling the events and in modelling the operations that follow events. Attributes are those elements which supply data to support the events. 'Tom' is an occurrence of the entity EMPLOYEE. Tom's pay rise or his sacking are events, and attributes of the entity EMPLOYEE will be referred to following these events. Attributes such as 'pay-to-date', 'tax-to-date', 'employment status', and 'salary' will be referred to. **Operations** on attributes will be necessary following the event: an event triggers an operation or a series of operations. An operation will change the state of the data. The event 'increase salary by 10%' will require access to the entity occurrence 'Tom' and augmenting the attribute, 'salary', by 10%. Figure 3.6 shows the entity EMPLOYEE expressed as a relation with attributes. Does the relation support all the operations that follow the event mentioned?

Employee

Employee

Empl. No.	Name	Status	Pay-to-date	Tax-to-date	Salary
756	Tom	Full	754.30	157.00	14000.00

Does the entity support the operations necessary following events?
    e.g. employee gets sacked
        employee gets a pay rise

Fig. 3.6. Event-driven (functional) analysis.

Some readers may be confused by the discussion of events (or transactions), which are function-oriented concepts, when data analysis is supposed to be function-independent. The events and operations are of interest as a checking mechanism. They are used to ensure that the entity model will support the functions. This consideration of the events and operations may lead to a tuning of the model, an adjustment of the entities and the attributes. This event-driven analysis is frequently called **functional analysis**.

Another possible source of confusion is the similarity of the terms 'relations' and 'relationships'. Whereas relationships express the association between two entities, relations are a tabular representation of an entity, complete with attributes. Although the two names are similar, they represent two distinct concepts.

3.4 PHASES IN ENTITY ANALYSIS

The phases in entity analysis are as follows:

> Define the area for analysis
>
> Define the entities and relationships
>
> Establish the key attribute(s) for each entity
>
> Complete each entity with all the attributes
>
> Normalise all the entities to third normal form
>
> Ensure all events and operations are supported by the model

The first stage of entity analysis requires the definition of the area for analysis. Sometimes this will be the organisation, but this is usually too ambitious for detailed study, and as we have seen the organisation will be divided into local areas for separate analysis.

For each local area, the entities are defined. The analyst will attempt to name the fundamental things of interest to the organisation. As the analyst is gathering these entities, the relationships between the entities can also be determined. These can be one-to-one, one-to-many, or many-to-many. It may be possible to identify fixed degree relationships. The analyst will also give a name to the relationship and begin to assemble the entity-relationship diagram. The diagram will be like a doodle in the beginning, but it will soon be useful as a communication tool. The key of each entity will also be determined. The key attributes will uniquely identify any entity occurrence.

The analyst has now obtained the model in outline and is in a position to fill in the detail. This means establishing the attributes for each entity. Each attribute will say something about the entity. The analyst has to ensure that any synonyms and homonyms are detected. A product could be called a part, product or finished product depending on the department. These are all synonyms for 'product'. On the other hand, the term product may mean different things (homonyms), depending on the department. It could mean a final saleable item in the marketing department or a sub-assembly in the production department. These differences must be reconciled and recorded in the data dictionary. Any data element in the organisation must be defined as an entity, an attribute or a relationship.

Each entity must be normalised to third normal form once the entity occurrences have been added to the model. This process is described in section 3.7. Briefly, the rules of normalisation require that all entries in the entity must be completed, all attributes of the entity must be dependent on all the key, and all non-key attributes must be independent of one another. The normalisation process may well lead to an increase in the number of relations/entities in the model. At the end of the process the entity model will show only the real data dependencies.

ENTITY DOCUMENT

Form No. .... Aliases	Entity name	Date	Analyst ....
Description			
Key		Size	
Attributes			
Relationships			
Data dictionary name .... Maximum No. of entries		Privacy level	
Notes			

Fig. 3.7. Entity documentation.

The final stage of the approach will be to look at all the events within the area and the operations that need to be performed following an event, and ensure that the model supports these events and operations. Events are frequently referred to as transactions. For this part of the methodology, the analyst will identify the events associated with the organisation and examine the operations necessary on the trail of each of the events.

Events in many organisations could include 'customer makes an order' and 'raw materials are purchased from supplier' and 'employee joins firm'. If, say, a customer makes an order, this event will be followed by a number of operations. The operations will be carried out in order to find out how much the order will cost, whether the product is in stock, and whether the customer's credit limit is OK. The entities such as PRODUCT (to look at the value of the attribute 'stock') and CUSTOMER (to look at the value of the attribute 'credit limit') must be examined (see below). These attribute values will need to be adjusted following the event. You may notice that the 'product price' is not in either entity. To support the event, therefore, 'product price' should be included in the PRODUCT entity, or in another entity which is brought into the model.

PRODUCT
Product No*
Product Description
Stock No*

CUSTOMER
Customer No*
Customer Name
Customer Address
Credit Limit*

* means referenced by
operations following events

Entity modelling has documentation aids like other methods of systems analysis. It is possible to obtain forms on which to specify all the elements of the data analysis process. The separate documents will enable the specification of entities, attributes, and relationships. It is shown in Figs 3.7, 3.8, 3.9, 3.10, and 3.1. Partially completed forms are shown in the Appendix.

ATTRIBUTE DOCUMENT

Form No.	Attribute name	Date	Analyst
···········	·····················	·········	···········
Aliases			
Description			

Data dictionary name	No. of chars.	Type	
·······························	·········	···························	

Range		No. occurrences	
·····························		·····························	

Validation	Privacy level
	·································

Defined in entities

Notes

Fig. 3.8. Attribute documentation.

It may be possible to use completed documents directly as input to a data dictionary system so that the data is held in a readily-accessible computer format as well as on paper forms. A description of data dictionaries is given in chapter 9.

Entity modelling is a communication tool as well as a technique for

RELATIONSHIP DOCUMENT

Form No.	Relationship	Date	Analyst
··········	···············	·········	·············
Description			
Identifier			
Type			
Frequency			
Privacy level			
Notes			

Fig. 3.9. Relationship documentation.

finding out information. The forms discussed help as an aid to memory — communication with oneself. The entity-relationship diagrams, which are particularly useful in the initial analysis and as an overview of the data model, prove a good basis for communication to managers. They are much more understandable to non-computer people than the documents used in conventional data processing. They provide a pictorial description of the business in outline, showing what the business *is*, NOT what it *does*. Managers can give 'user feedback' to the data analysts and this will also help to tune the model and ensure its accuracy. A manager may point out that an attribute is missing from an entity, or that a relationship between entities is one-to-many and not one-to-

EVENT DOCUMENT

Form No.	Event name	Date	Analyst
....	....	....	....

Description

Frequency	Operations following event

Entity	Privacy level
....	....

Pathway following event

Notes

Fig. 3.10. Event documentation.

one as implied by the entity-relationship diagram. The manager may not use this terminology, but the data analyst will be able to interpret his comments. Data analysis is a reiterative process: the final model will not be obtained until after a number of tries and this should not be seen as slowness, but care for accuracy. If the entity model is inaccurate so will be the data base and the applications that use it.

The entity-relationship diagram given in Fig. 3.12 shows the entities for part of a firm of wholesalers. Included in the figure are the attributes of the entities. The key attributes are *underlined*. Perhaps you would like to verify that you can understand something of the organisation using this form of documentation. It is a first sketch of the business, and

OPERATION DOCUMENT

Form No.	Operation name	Date	Analyst
....	....	....	....
Description			
Access key			
Entities			
Events			
Response time			
Frequency	Privacy level		
Notes			

Fig. 3.11. Operation documentation.

you may also verify the relationships, add entities and relationships to the model or attributes to the entities, so that the model is more appropriate for a typical firm of wholesalers. For example, I have not included payments in this interim model.

3.5 ALTERNATIVE APPROACHES TO DATA ANALYSIS

The entity-relationship approach to data analysis is **interview-driven**, that is most information is obtained through interviewing members of staff. An alternative approach is **document-driven**, where most of the information comes from a study of documents. These documents could

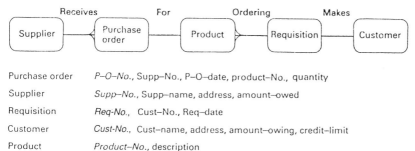

Purchase order	P–O–No., Supp–No., P–O–date, product–No., quantity	
Supplier	Supp–No., Supp–name, address, amount–owed	
Requisition	Req-No., Cust–No., Req–date	
Customer	Cust-No., Cust–name, address, amount–owing, credit–limit	
Product	Product–No., description	

Fig. 3.12. Entity-relationship diagram — a first approach for a wholesaler.

be the input forms used in the system and output reports, both hard copy and soft copy designs. In order to make the model flexible, the investigation will include reports likely to be required in the future.

Though this approach includes a formal technique to derive the model, other information gathered in the investigation phase can be incorporated in the final model so derived. The methodology has the following steps:

(1) Identify the documents that most typify the area under investigation. Each of these is processed in turn, starting with the most significant. These are usually the ones that carry most data.

(2) Identify the data elements on these documents and attach names to each of these. Ensure that synonyms and homonyms are recognised. This may well necessitate interviewing people in the department concerned. Construct and develop the data dictionary.

(3) Draw data usage diagrams for each of these documents. These diagrams highlight the relationships that the documents reflect, in particular any hierarchical structure that the document shows.

(4) Separate each level of the diagram as a relation with attributes. Find the identifying (or key) attributes. Modify the relations so that they conform to the rules of normalisation.

(5) Combine the relations obtained in the present document with the set obtained from previous documents. This may imply adding new relations to the set, adding data elements (attributes) to one or more of the relations, or breaking up one relation into others. As more and more documents are processed, the less likely will subsequent documents effect a change in the overall model.

The methodology is best illustrated by an example which is taken from Avison (1981). Figure 3.13 shows an online enquiry and its associated **Data Usage Diagram** (DUD). The first level of the DUD relates to jobs and the second level to orders for parts, because for each occurrence of the job data, there can be many occurrences of orders data. Therefore the relations JOB and ORDERS are as follows (with key attributes underlined):

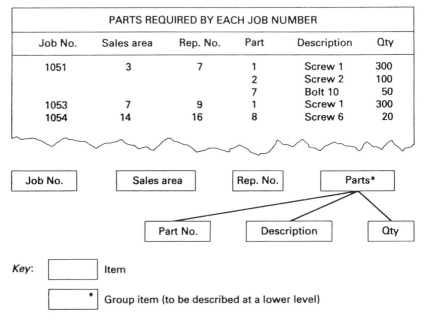

PARTS REQUIRED BY EACH JOB NUMBER					
Job No.	Sales area	Rep. No.	Part	Description	Qty
1051	3	7	1	Screw 1	300
			2	Screw 2	100
			7	Bolt 10	50
1053	7	9	1	Screw 1	300
1054	14	16	8	Screw 6	20

Key: [   ] Item

[*] Group item (to be described at a lower level)

Fig. 3.13. Forming data usage diagram from output document.

JOB   (*Job-number*, sales-area, representative-number)

ORDERS   (*Job-number*, *part-number*, part-description, quantity-ordered)

Figure 3.14 gives another report to be analysed and its DUD. This shows that for each sales area there may be a number of representatives. The JOB relation will have to be modified and a SALES relation formed.

JOB   (*Job-number*, sales-area)

SALES   (*Sales-area*, *representative-number*, sales-amount)

The process is continued, developing and tuning the set of relations, until all the documents have been analysed. In practice, it is rarely

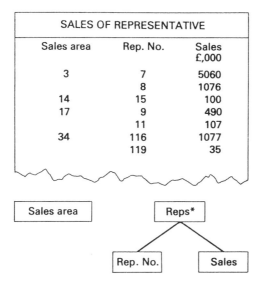

SALES OF REPRESENTATIVE		
Sales area	Rep. No.	Sales £,000
3	7	5060
	8	1076
14	15	100
17	9	490
	11	107
34	116	1077
	119	35

Fig. 3.14. Analysing another document.

possible to thoroughly analyse all the documents of the organisation in this way. The process is too slow. The first few documents will be used to create the initial model. Later documents will be perused rather than analysed to ensure that no new information is revealed.

The major criticism of this approach is that it assumes that all information about the organisation is kept in documents. For this reason it is best to consider the approach document 'driven'. In other words, whilst analysing documents, other information, such as that gained from interviews, can be incorporated into the model. A knowledge of the firm could soon reveal that the 'part-description' in the ORDERS relation is dependent on the 'part-number', not the whole key. This does not conform to the rules of normalisation (attributes must give facts about all the key). There should therefore be another relation formed relating to PARTS, and the ORDERS relation modified.

PARTS   (*Part-number*, part-description)

ORDERS   (*Job-number, part-number*, quantity-ordered)

This approach can be used to verify the model obtained from an entity-relationship or another approach. A further approach, also a data collection approach, works by collecting the facts of interest to the enterprise. The attributes are then combined into normalised relations. Like the Data Collection Approach, but unlike the entity-relationship approach, it is a **bottom-up** procedure. The entity-relationship approach looks at the major things of interest first. This is a **top-down** technique. Although bottom-up approaches work for simple cases, there usually proves to be too large a number of attributes to analyse in more realistic situations.

3.6 RELATIONAL MODELLING

In 1970 Ted Codd published his influential paper 'A Relational Model for Large Shared Data Banks'. This has had a profound effect on systems analysis and data base design. Most of the early work in data processing had been done pragmatically with developments taking place in the data processing applications environment rather than in the research and academic environments. Little or no formal techniques were being used or developed: problems were solved by rule of thumb and guesswork.

However, by the 1970s the early pioneering days of computer data processing were over and more sophisticated integrated systems were being developed. Large integrated files were needed. Customer files, for example, were being developed which included data relevant to more than one system. These could include sales order, sales ledger and bad debt processing. Later came data bases. Codd's research was directed at a very real problem, that is the deletion, insertion and update of data on these very large files.

Being a mathematician, his approach to the problem was mathematical. The relational model offers mathematical formalism and thus has a sound theoretical foundation even though it is fairly new in the field of data modelling. In describing the work in this text, however, it is intended to avoid a formal mathematical treatment.

The relational model is stressed in this text for a number of reasons:

The model is understandable by users as well as technologists

The model is readily transferable into other data models

The model is not computer oriented

The model is not biased towards particular user requirements

The model is readily derived by the processes of data analysis

Different users can see different views of the model

It is a model which is *readily understandable* by the technologists, and also, more importantly, by managers and users. They can far more readily appreciate the meaning of the data relationships illustrated in a tabular form than they could in the file and record specification forms of conventional systems analysis. These are computer-oriented. I have found more difficulty teaching the relational model to computer students (who want to think in terms of computer jargon and are looking for complications that do not exist) than to management students. It is not necessary to know anything of computers or computer file structures to understand the relational model and to use it. Everyone has used tables, and relations are tables.

Relations are *readily transformable* into other models, such as hierarchies or networks, which are often but not exclusively the ways in which data base management systems require the data structures to be presented. Increasingly, relational data base management systems are being used. These systems expect data to be presented to it in terms of relations and normally present results to users in the form of relations.

The relational model is *not computer oriented*. It is not biased by any particular physical storage structure that may be used. The model stays the same whether the storage structures are held on magnetic tape, disk, or main storage. It is not biased towards the way that the data may be accessed from storage media. If the target system is a computer system, it could be mainframe, minicomputer or microcomputer.

It *does not show bias towards particular users*: either particular user enquiries, enquiry types, or the enquiries from a particular (perhaps powerful) user. Many systems make some questions easier to ask and answer, particularly where the structure of these matches the design of the data base. This is not true of the relational model. The data base administrator may choose to optimise the performance of some query type which is posed frequently, but these considerations are not made when building the data model.

The relational model can be *readily derived from data analysis*. Most data analysis techniques derive their data model as a set of relations. It maintains the truths of the universe it represents. Thus it can accurately represent that part of the real world that was modelled in the data analysis process. It can also be adapted to reflect changes in the organisation and 'readily adapted', if the relations have been normalised (because normalisation leads to a much more flexible model).

Although the model represents the organisation as a whole, it can be adapted so that a particular part of the model can appear in a *different form to different users*. There will be one overall model, the conceptual schema, but in the logical model, the various user views can be represented as **sub-schemas** (particular user views). Such flexibility allows users to see that part of the data model that interests them and avoid another wise over-complicated view of the model and support other requirements such as privacy and security.

As seen in Fig. 3.15, a relation is a flat file. This relation is called ORDER and it could show that Lee ordered 12 of 'part number' 25, Deene and Smith ordered 18 and 9 respectively of 'part number' 38, and Williams ordered 100 of 'part number' 87.

ORDER

NAME	PART	QUANTITY
LEE	25	12
DEENE	38	18
SMITH	38	9
WILLIAMS	87	100

Fig. 3.15. Relation 'ORDER'.

Each row is called a **tuple**. The order of tuples is immaterial, although they will normally be shown in the text in key sequence so that you can follow their contents easier. No two tuples can be identical in the model. A tuple will have a number of **attributes**, and in the ORDER relation, 'name', 'part' and 'quantity' are attributes. All items in a column come from the same **domain** — there are circumstances where the contents from two or more columns come from the same domain. The relation ELECTION RESULT illustrates this possibility. Two attributes come from the same domain of Political Parties. The number of attributes in a relation is called the **degree** of the relation. A relation with two attributes is known as a binary relation. The number of tuples in a relation define its **cardinality**.

ELECTION-RESULT

ELECTION YEAR	FIRST PARTY	SECOND PARTY
1972	LABOUR	CONSERVATIVE
1974	LABOUR	CONSERVATIVE
1979	CONSERVATIVE	LABOUR
1983	CONSERVATIVE	LABOUR

Fig. 3.16. Relation 'ELECTION RESULT'.

Each tuple is distinguished from another because one or more attributes in a relation are designated **key attributes**. In the ORDER relation, the key is 'name', and it is *underlined* in the column. It might be better to allocate numbers to customers in case there are duplicate names. If the customer may make orders for a number of parts, then 'part' must also be a key attribute. 'Name' and 'part' will make up the **composite key** of the ORDER relation. What is the key for the ELECTION RESULT relation? On first sight, 'election year' would seem appropriate, but there may be two elections in a year. Even if all three attributes were part of the key, this could still bring about duplicate relations as there could be two elections in the same year giving the same result. It is necessary to add another attribute or replace 'year' by 'election date' (there will not be two elections of the same type in the same day) to make each tuple unique. Alternatively the composite key 'election year' and 'election number in year' will be adequate. There may be more than one possible key. These are known as **candidate keys**. In this circumstance one of these is chosen as the **primary key**.

The structure of the relation is conventionally expressed as follows:

ORDER (*name*, part, quantity) and

ELECTION-RESULT (*elect-year*, *elect-number*, first-party, second-party)

3.7 NORMALISATION

The process of normalisation is the application of a number of rules to the relational model which will simplify the relations. These rules prove to be a useful guideline because we are dealing with large sets of data and the relations formed by the normalisation process will make the data easier to understand and manipulate. This means that the design of languages to manipulate relations will also be less complex. As well as simplifying the relations, normalisation also clears anomolies which may otherwise occur when manipulating them.

Codd developed three nested levels of normalisation, and the third and final stage is known as **Third Normal Form** (TNF). It is this level of normalisation that is usually used as the basis for the design of the data model, as an end result of data analysis, and for mapping onto a data base (the logical schema). There are a few instances, however, when even TNF needs further simplification, and Kent (1983) develops normalisation further. TNF is usually satisfactory and the model is not developed further in this text. The stages of normalisation are described differently in a number of texts, but I have found that the following descriptions of the stages work well in practice:

FIRST NORMAL FORM   Ensure that all the attributes are atomic (in the smallest possible components), that is there is only one value for each domain and not a set of values.

SECOND NORMAL
            FORM

Ensure that all non-key attributes are functionally dependent on (give facts about) *all* the key. Split off those attributes that are dependent on only part of the key.

THIRD NORMAL FORM

Ensure that all non-key attributes are functionally *in*dependent of each other. Create new relations so that these do not show any non-key dependence.

The process of normalisation is only made possible by an understanding of the real relationships in the organisation, otherwise assumptions have to be made which may be incorrect. A rather flippant definition of normalisation can be given as 'the attributes in a relation depend on the key, the whole key, and nothing but the key'. This is an oversimplification, but it is essentially true and could be kept in mind as normalisation is developed.

Functional dependency is defined by Cardenas (1983) as follows:

> Given a relation R, the attribute B is said to be functionally dependent on attribute A if at every instant of time each value of A has no more than one value of B associated with it in the relation R.

Functional dependency is frequently illustrated by an arrow. The arrow will point from A to B in the functional dependency illustrated in the definition. Thus, the value of A uniquely determines the value of B.

$$A \longrightarrow B$$

Before normalising the relation given as Fig. 3.17, it is necessary to analyse the meaning of the relation. Knowledge of the application area gained from data analysis will provide this information. It is possible to make assumptions about the inter-relationships between the data, but it is obviously better to base these assumptions on thorough analysis. In the relation COURSE-DETAILS, there are two occurrences of 'course', one numbered B74 called computer science at the B.Sc. level and the other B75 called computer applications at the M.Sc. level. Each of these 'courses' has a number of 'modules' associated with it. Each 'module' is given a 'name', 'status' and 'unit-points' (which are allocated

RELATION COURSE-DETAILS

COURSE	C-NAME	LEVEL	MODULE	NAME	STATUS	UNIT-POINTS
B74	Comp.Sci.	B.Sc.	B741	Programming 1	Basic	8
			B742	Hardware 1		
			B743	Data Proc. 1		
			B744	Programming 2	Int.	11
			B745	Hardware 2		
B95	Comp.Apps.	M.Sc.	B951	Adv.Prog.	Adv.	15
			B952	Micros.		

Filling in the details is a trivial task:

COURSE DETAILS

COURSE	C-NAME	LEVEL	MODULE	NAME	STATUS	UNIT-POINTS
B74	Comp.Sci.	B.Sc.	B741	Programming 1	Basic	8
B74	Comp.Sci.	B.Sc.	B742	Hardware 1	Basic	8
B74	Comp.Sci.	B.Sc.	B743	Data Proc. 1	Basic	8
B74	Comp.Sci.	B.Sc.	B744	Programming 2	Int.	11
B74	Comp.Sci.	B.Sc.	B745	Hardware 2	Int.	11
B95	Comp.Apps.	M.Sc.	B951	Adv.Prog.	Adv.	15
B95	Comp.Apps.	M.Sc.	B952	Micros.	Adv.	15

Fig. 3.17. First normal form.

according to the status of the 'module'). 'Course' number and 'module' number form the composite key.

First Normal Form: First and second normal forms are stages towards arriving at third normal form. The first stage of normalisation includes the filling in of details. This is seen in the example in Fig. 3.17 and is a trivial task. You may note that in Fig. 3.17, the order of the tuples in the unnormalised relation at the top is significant. Otherwise the content of the uncompleted attributes cannot be known. As we have discussed, one of the principles of the relational model is that the order of the tuples should *not* be significant.

Further work would have been necessary if the following was presented as the unnormalised relation:

COURSE C-NAME LEVEL MODULE-DETAILS

'Module-details' has to be defined as a set of atomic attributes, not as a group item, thus:

COURSE C-NAME LEVEL MODULE NAME STATUS UNIT-POINTS

will be the result in first normal form, with all the details filled out.

Second Normal Form: Second normal form is achieved if the relations are in first normal form and all non-key attributes are fully functionally dependent on all the key. In the relation COURSE-DETAILS, which is in first normal form, the attributes 'status', 'name' and 'unit-points' are functionally dependent on 'module', in other words they represent facts about 'module', which is only part of the key. They are not dependent on the other part of the key, 'course'. Two relations will therefore be formed from the relation shown as Fig. 3.18.

But the relation COURSE-MODULE is still not in second normal form because the attributes 'c-name' and 'level' are functionally dependent on 'course'. A separate COURSE relation has been created in Fig. 3.19. So as to avoid tuples being the same, the COURSE relation has only two tuples (there are only two courses). Notice that we maintain a relation COURSE-MODULE. This relation is all key, and there is nothing incorrect in this. Attributes may be added later which relate specifically to the *module-course* relationship. The relation is maintained because information will be lost by not including it, specifically the modules which are included in a particular course.

Third Normal Form: Second normal form may cause problems where non-key attributes are functionally dependent on each other (a non-key

COURSE-MODULE

COURSE	MODULE	C-NAME	LEVEL
B74	B741	Comp.Sci.	B.Sc.
B74	B742	Comp.Sci.	B.Sc.
B74	B743	Comp.Sci.	B.Sc.
B74	B744	Comp.Sci.	B.Sc.
B74	B745	Comp.Sci.	B.Sc.
B95	B951	Comp.Apps.	M.Sc.
B95	B952	Comp.Apps.	M.Sc.

MODULE

MODULE	NAME	STATUS	UNIT-POINTS
B741	Programming 1	Basic	8
B742	Hardware 1	Basic	8
B743	Data Proc. 1	Basic	8
B744	Programming 2	Int.	11
B745	Hardware 2	Int.	11
B751	Adv.Prog.	Adv.	15
B752	Micros	Adv.	15

Fig. 3.18. Towards second normal form — course-module needs further normalisation.

attribute is dependent on another non-key attribute). This is resolved by converting the relations into TNF. In the relation MODULE, the attribute 'unit-points' is functionally dependent on the 'status' (or level) of the course. We create a new relation STATUS and delete 'unit-points' from the relation MODULE. The third normal form is given in Fig. 3.20.

Sometimes the term **transitive dependency** is used in this context. The dependency of the attribute 'unit-points' is transitive (via 'status') and not wholly dependent on the key attribute 'module'. This transitive dependency should not exist in third normal form.

Some of you may have realised that 'status' is dependent on 'module-name' as well as 'module'. (We will assume for this purpose that every 'module-name' is unique.) This is correct because if all 'module-names' are unique, then 'module' and 'module-name' are candidate keys. Dependency of non-key attributes to a candidate key is allowable in TNF, but it must be a candidate key. The attribute 'status' is not a candidate key in the relation MODULE, and therefore the STATUS relation needs to be created for TNF.

MODULE

MODULE	NAME	STATUS	UNIT-POINTS
B741	Programming 1	Basic	8
B742	Hardware 1	Basic	8
B743	Data Proc. 1	Basic	8
B744	Programming 2	Int.	11
B745	Hardware 2	Int.	11
B751	Adv.Prog.	Adv.	15
B752	Micros	Adv.	15

COURSE-MODULE

COURSE	MODULE
B74	B741
B74	B742
B74	B743
B74	B744
B74	B745
B95	B951
B95	B952

COURSE

COURSE	C-NAME	LEVEL
B74	Comp.Sci.	B.Sc.
B95	Comp.Apps.	M.Sc.

Fig. 3.19. Second normal form.

Computer packages are becoming available which are designed to help analysts convert data into third normal form relations. One such product is the software house LBMS's product Workbench.

Why Normalise?: Relations are normalised because unnormalised relations prove difficult to use. This can be illustrated if we try to insert, delete, and update information from the relations not in TNF. Say we have a new 'module' numbered B985 called Artificial Intelligence and which has a 'status' in the intermediate category. Looking at Fig. 3.17,

COURSE-MODULE

COURSE	MODULE
B74	B741
B74	B742
B74	B743
B74	B744
B74	B745
B95	B951
B95	B952

COURSE

COURSE	C-NAME	LEVEL
B74	Comp.Sci.	B.Sc.
B95	Comp.Apps.	M.Sc.

MODULE

MODULE	NAME	STATUS
B741	Programming 1	Basic
B742	Hardware 1	Basic
B743	Data Proc. 1	Basic
B744	Programming 2	Int.
B745	Hardware 2	Int.
B951	Adv.Prog.	Adv.
B952	Micros	Adv.

STATUS

STATUS	UNIT-POINTS
Basic	8
Int.	11
Adv.	15

Fig. 3.20. Third normal form.

we cannot add this information in COURSE-DETAILS because there has been no allocation of this 'module' occurrence to any 'course'.

Looking at Fig. 3.18, it could be added to the MODULE relation, if we knew that the 'status' intermediate carried 11 unit-points. This information is not necessary in the MODULE relation seen in Fig. 3.20, the TNF version of this relation. The TNF model is therefore much more convenient for adding the new information.

If we decided to introduce a new category in the 'status' attribute, called coursework, having a 'unit-points' attached of 10, we cannot add it to the relation MODULE (Fig. 3.18) because we have not decided which 'module' or modules to attach it to. But we can include this information in the TNF model by adding a tuple to the STATUS relation (Fig. 3.20).

Another problem occurs when updating. Let us say that we decide to change the 'unit-points' allocated to the Basic category of 'status' in the modules from 8 to 6, it becomes a simple matter in the TNF module. The single occurrence of the tuple with the key Basic, needs to be changed from (Basic 8) to (Basic 6). With the unnormalised, first normal or second normal form relations, there will be a number of tuples to change. It means searching through every tuple of the relation COURSE-DETAILS (Fig. 3.17) or MODULE (Fig. 3.18) looking for 'status' = Basic and updating the associated 'unit-points'. All tuples have to be searched for, because in the relational model the order of the tuples is of no significance. I have ordered them to make them easier for the reader to follow.

Deleting information will also cause problems. If it is decided to drop the B95 course, we may still wish to keep details of the modules which make up the course. Information about modules might be used at another time when designing another course. The information would be lost if we deleted the course B95 from COURSE-DETAILS (Fig. 3.17). The information about these modules will be retained in the MODULE relation in TNF. The TNF relation COURSE will now consist only of one tuple:

COURSE	C-NAME	LEVEL
B74	Comp.Sci.	B.Sc.

REFERENCES

Avison, D.E. (1981) 'Techniques of Data Analysis', *Computer Bulletin*, **II**/29.
    A short introduction to some techniques of data analysis.

Cardenas, A.F. (1985) *Data Base Management Systems* (2nd edn). Allyn and Bacon, Boston.

A good introduction to data bases. The definition of functional dependency is given on page 497.

Chen, P.P.S. (1976) 'The Entity-Relationship Model — Toward a Unified View of Data', *ACM Transactions on Database Systems*, **1**.

This paper was an early statement of the E-R approach.

Codd, E.F. (1970) 'A Relational Model of Data for Large Shared Data Banks', *Communications of the ACM*, **13**.

Codd defined in this and other papers the basic tenets of normalisation theory.

Howe, D.R. (1983) *Data Analysis for Data Base Design*. Arnold, London.

A good basic text on data analysis.

Kent, W. (1983) 'A Simple Guide to Five Normal Forms in Relational Theory', *Communications of the ACM*, **26**, .

The title of this paper is self-explanatory and fair.

Robinson, H. (1981) *Database Analysis and Design*. Chartwell-Bratt, Bromley.

Covers the relational and E-R approaches to data analysis.

Veryard, R. (1984) *Pragmatic Data Analysis*. Blackwell Scientific, Oxford.

A commonsense, practical approach to data analysis.

Chapter 4

The Logical Schema
Relational, Hierarchical and Network Views

4.1 INTRODUCTION

Having formed an agreed conceptual schema, a model which represents the enterprise and is independent of any type of physical system (computer or otherwise), it is possible to transfer or 'map' this model on to a data base management system (DBMS). The use of a DBMS is not necessary in general, but it is part of the methodology for implementing information systems discussed in this text. Thus the entity model is mapped into a form required by the particular DBMS used. This is the **logical schema**. Most DBMS require the data structures to be presented in one of three ways: as relations, hierarchies, or networks. Although most DBMS fall into one of these design types, some do not. This will be looked at in chapter 7 where a number of commercial DBMS are investigated. Some writers distinguish a fourth type of data base, the inverted file. This distinction is more related to the physical schema (the next stage of developing the data model) and a discussion of inverted files is therefore given in chapter 5.

It should be emphasised that the data model which we have called the conceptual schema was developed independently of both machine and software considerations. It represents the integrated user views of the data and the data relationships in the area chosen. This means than an 'ideal' data model can be formulated with the knowledge that it can be mapped on to a DBMS. Its conversion to a logical schema can then be made and this will be in the form required by the target DBMS. Some DBMS accept more than one data model type, for example both relations and hierarchies. The accuracy of the mapping from conceptual schema to logical schema is crucial to the success of the data base project: there should be no loss of information.

In order to put this mapping of conceptual to logical schema into perspective (and therefore the place of this chapter in the overall methodology), the next step (discussed in chapter 5) is a further mapping to the storage level representation of data. However this mapping will be largely transparent to the user, in other words the DBMS will take care of physical mapping onto storage media and file organisation. This may

88

be carried out using instructions from the data base administrator, who will choose between the alternative file organisation methods offered (if any) by the DBMS as appropriate for the particular data. This may be achieved by linked lists, indexes, inverted files, random access or other methods of file organisation. This is the concern of the physical schema. DBMS therefore have two views of the data: the logical schema, which is the view given to it by the user, programmer or data base administrator, and the physical schema. The position of the DBMS, acting as a cushion between the logical views of the data structure and the physical schema, is shown in Fig. 4.1.

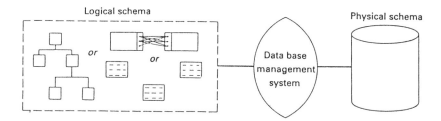

Fig. 4.1. The logical schema and the data base management system.

Ingres, IMS and IDMS are DBMS giving examples of each data base type. Ingres is a relational DBMS, that is data structures are presented to it in the form of tables; IMS views the data structures in terms of hierarchies; and IDMS in terms of networks. This chapter discusses these forms of the logical schema. It looks at the basics of relations, hierarchies and networks, and also shows how the data structures might be described to the data base. This description is usually called the **Data Definition Language** (DDL) of the particular DBMS. An introduction to a DDL for each type of system is discussed below along with a description of the ways in which the data could be accessed and updated using the **Data Manipulation Language** (DML). These features will be developed further in chapter 7 when we look at particular DBMS.

4.2 THE RELATIONAL APPROACH

The relational model was described in chapter 3 and therefore it is not proposed to repeat this description here. The model is an excellent means of describing the data structures in an enterprise, independently of the requirements of a particular DBMS or any other computer-oriented factor. Many DBMS, such as Rapport, Ingres, DB/2, dBaseIII and Info, are relational systems, and therefore can take advantage of the particular features of the relational structure. This does not mean that the logical model need be a relational one, but it is obviously convenient to use a relational DBMS when using the methology described in the text.

When converting the conceptual schema to the relational model, entities become relations (entity occurrences being the tuples); the attributes are mapped directly, the key attributes of an entity will be the same as those of the relation; the relationships also become relations, their keys being derived from the keys of the two relations taking part in the relationship. The result is a set of normalised relations mapped on to the target DBMS.

Though the conceptual schema will be a set of relations normalised to third normal form, it may be efficient to have a logical design specified to the DBMS which has some non-normalised relations. If a particular group item is always associated by users with a relation, it may be reasonable to specify a non-normalised relation. This will be, a decision of the data base administrator. Relations may also be stored which are *derived* from the primary set of relations. Thus, from a basic Employee relation

EMPLOYEE   (emp-num, emp-name, dept-num)

and a basic Department relation of

DEPARTMENT   (dept-num, dept-name, no-of-staff, head)

an Employee details relation consisting of

EMPLOYEE-DETAILS   (emp-num, enp-name, dept-num, dept-name, dept-head)

may be derived. There may be good grounds, such as frequent access, to include this non-TNF and derived relation on the data base. The derived relations will be formed using the relational Data Manipulation Language (DML) of the DBMS. The DML is the data base language which is used to join relations together and pick out selected tuples or domains as requested by the user.

In most DBMS, tables are easy to create. The DBMS may have a CREATE command, such as:

    CREATE RELATION EMPLOYEE
    (EMP-NUM,10,N

EMP-NAME,30,C
CREDIT-LIM,5,N)

This will set up the structure of a relation called EMPLOYEE which has three attributes. The 'employee number' is a 10 digit number, the 'employee name' is 30 characters long, and the 'credit limit' is a 5 digit number. No links need be set up in a relational data base between relations. The links are set up temporarily by the DBMS when a relational operator is effected. This operator will be part of the DML.

One of the most interesting aspects of relational data bases are their data manipulation languages. Codd (1970) developed a series of operators to manipulate relations. These operators include those to merge relations and to separate out some columns or some rows. The set of operators are known together as the **Relational Algebra**. Other DMLs such as the Relational Calculus are usually translated into relational algebra by the system before executing the request on the data base. The relational algebra is a procedural language. The operators manipulate the relations using a series of steps to perform the user's requirements. The relational calculus is non-procedural, and the data base system is expected to translate this into procedural steps.

In a relational system, the result of any operation on one or more relations is itself a relation. This gives the relational model advantages over other models. The language reflects the design of the system. The DML can also be **relationally complete**: it is possible to perform any data manipulation on the relations required by the user using one or more of the relational algebra operators. The language is also executed dynamically. In other words the access paths for joining or separating relations is not set up with the data. It is set up each time the operation is required. This has particular advantages where the user requests are not predictable, but less efficient when compared to hierarchical and network systems in situations where the access paths are predictable and therefore can be set up beforehand and executed each time it is required. For this reason, many relational DBMS do give the DBA the opportunity to set up indexes at data creation time so as to increase the speed by which data is retrieved. We now look at the relational algebra and the relational calculus in more detail. Many DML implementations are based on one of these specifications.

Relational Algebra

The relational algebra is a collection of operators on relations. It includes the traditional set operators union, intersection, difference and product. The UNION of two relations is the set of all tuples belonging to either or both of the relations. The INTERSECTION of two relations is the set of all tuples belonging to both of the relations. The DIFFERENCE of two relations is the set of all tuples belonging to one relation but not the other. Thus A MINUS B is the set of tuples belonging to relation A and not B. The PRODUCT of two relations concatenates each pair of tuples on the original tables. Thus, if the first table has R rows and the second table r rows, then the product of the two relations will be R×r rows. This operator is infrequently used because it is indiscriminate in the way it joins tuples together. (Usually the JOIN operator is more appropriate, as we shall see later in this section.) These are all traditional set operators and they require that all relations included in one operation have the same **degree**, that is, they have the same number of columns. This requirement is sometimes referred to as **union compatability**.

So as to illustrate the use of these operators, we will consider the three relations in Fig. 4.2. They give information about an M.Sc. course which consists of four parts, three of which have a ten week compulsory unit and a choice of options. The STUDENT relation contains the name of the student and the particular year of the course he is on. Part-time students take two years to complete the course. The relation LECTUR-ER-MODULE gives the module number (each compulsory unit and option is termed a module) the name of the lecturer presenting the module and the number of weeks it lasts. One course has no options, it runs the full 20 weeks. Finally, ATTENDANCE gives the student name, the modules that he has chosen and the lecturer of that module. The reader will realise that the relations are not in third normal form.

Consider the ATTENDANCE relation. If A is the set of students attending module 3, and B is the set of students attending module 2a (see Fig. 4.3a), then

    A UNION B

is the set of students tuples (Fig. 4.3b) who attend either module 3 or 2a (or both); and

    A INTERSECT B

will be the set of student tuples (Fig. 4.3c) who attend both module 3 and 2a. The DIFFERENCE between the two relations

RELATION: STUDENT

STUDENT-NAME	YEAR-OF-COURSE
Ashworth	1
Atkins	1
Johnson	2
Smith	1
Perkins	2

RELATION: LECTURER-MODULE

MODULE	LECTURER-NAME	NO-OF-WEEKS
1	Clarke	10
1a	Goodwin	10
1b	Goodwin	10
2	Knight	10
2a	Collins	10
2b	Baker	10
2c	Jagger	10
3	Fisher	10
3a	Oldham	10
4	Glenn	20

RELATION: ATTENDANCE

STUDENT-NAME	MODULE	LECTURER-NAME
Ashworth	1	Clarke
Ashworth	1b	Goodwin
Ashworth	2	Knight
Ashworth	2a	Collins
Ashworth	3	Fisher
Ashworth	3a	Oldham
Ashworth	4	Glenn
Atkins	1	Clarke
Atkins	1a	Goodwin
Atkins	2	Knight
Atkins	2b	Baker
Atkins	3	Fisher
Atkins	3a	Oldham
Atkins	4	Glenn
Johnson	1	Clarke
Johnson	1a	Goodwin
Johnson	2	Knight
Johnson	2c	Jagger
Smith	1	Clarke
Smith	1b	Goodwin
Smith	2a	Collins
Smith	3	Fisher
Smith	3a	Oldham
Smith	4	Glenn
Perkins	3	Fisher
Perkins	3a	Oldham
Perkins	4	Glenn

Fig. 4.2. The relations associated with an M.Sc. course.

A

STUDENT-NAME	MODULE	LECTURER-NAME
Ashworth	3	Fisher
Atkins	3	Fisher
Smith	3	Fisher
Perkins	3	Fisher

(a)

B

STUDENT-NAME	MODULE	LECTURER-NAME
Ashworth	2a	Collins
Smith	2a	Collins

(b) Result of union

STUDENT-NAME	MODULE	LECTURER-NAME
Ashworth	3	Fisher
Atkins	3	Fisher
Smith	3	Fisher
Perkins	3	Fisher
Ashworth	2a	Collins
Smith	2a	Collins

(c) Result of intersect

STUDENT-NAME	MODULE	LECTURER-NAME
Ashworth	3	Fisher
Smith	3	Fisher
Ashworth	2a	Collins
Smith	2a	Collins

(d) Result of minus

STUDENT-NAME	MODULE	LECTURER-NAME
Atkins	3	Fisher
Perkins	3	Fisher

Fig. 4.3. Results of operations on relations.

A MINUS B

will be the set of tuples (Fig. 4.3d) who attend module 3 but not module 2a.

Such operations may be useful for timetabling, classroom allocation and for making examination arrangements. The results are in tabular form and are therefore understandable to the user.

Some operations in the relational algebra are not traditional set operators, for example, PROJECT, SELECT and JOIN. The SELECT operator allows a choice to be made of the tuples in a relation. It takes a horizontal subset of an existing table. For example:

SELECT ATTENDANCE WHERE MODULE = 3a

will derive the relation shown as Fig. 4.4. The part of the statement 'WHERE MODULE = 3a', is called the **conditional** part of the statement.

STUDENT	MODULE	LECTURER-NAME
Ashworth	3a	Oldham
Atkins	3a	Oldham
Smith	3a	Oldham
Perkins	3a	Oldham

Fig. 4.4. Result of SELECT.

The statement:

SELECT LECTURER-MODULE WHERE NO-OF-WEEKS GREATER THAN 10

will give a one tuple relation:

MODULE	LECTURER-NAME	NO-OF-WEEKS
4	Glenn	20

The PROJECT operator will choose specified attributes of a relation and eliminate others. It therefore forms a vertical subset of an existing table by extracting columns. It also removes any duplicate tuples that may have been formed by the operation. Hence:

PROJECT LECTURER-MODULE OVER MODULE,
NO-OF-WEEKS

will give the relation shown in Fig. 4.5a. The PROJECT operator may also be used to change the order of attributes written in the relation, for example:

PROJECT LECTURER-MODULE OVER NO-OF-WEEKS,
MODULE

will give the relation shown as Fig. 4.5b.

MODULE	NO-OF-WEEKS
1	10
1a	10
1b	10
2	10
2a	10
2b	10
2c	10
3a	10
4	20

NO-OF-WEEKS	MODULE
10	1
10	1a
10	1b
10	2
10	2a
10	2b
10	2c
10	3a
20	4

(a)   (b)

Fig. 4.5. Result of PROJECTS.

The JOIN operator will produce a relation from two others where
there is the same value in a common domain. The result of a JOIN
operation is a new wider table in which each row is formed by concate-
nating the two rows that have the same value in the common domain.
For example:

JOIN LECTURER-MODULE AND ATTENDANCE OVER
MODULE

will result in Fig. 4.6. In some relational systems, the operation will be
written as:

JOIN LECTURER-MODULE AND ATTENDANCE
WHERE MODULE=MODULE

and some less refined systems repeat information in the relation that is
derived from the operation so that the result is a relation consisting of
the following columns:

MODULE LECTURER-NAME NO-OF-WEEKS
STUDENT-NAME MODULE LECTURER-NAME

In its simplest form, DIVISION is defined as an operation between a
binary relation (the dividend) and a unary relation (the divisor) which
produces a unary relation (the quotient) as its result. To form a binary

MODULE	LECTURER-NAME	NO.OF WEEKS	STUDENT-NAME
1	Clarke	10	Ashworth
1	Clarke	10	Atkins
1	Clarke	10	Johnson
1	Clarke	10	Smith
1a	Goodwin	10	Atkins
1a	Goodwin	10	Johnson
1b	Goodwin	10	Ashworth
1b	Goodwin	10	Ashworth
2	Knight	10	Ashworth

Fig. 4.6. Result of JOIN (part).

relation consisting of student-name and module, we first carry out a projection:

PROJECT ATTENDANCE OVER STUDENT-NAME AND
MODULE GIVING DEND

which will produce Fig. 4.7a. Let the divisor DDR be Fig. 4.7b, then:

DIVIDE DEND BY DDR OVER MODULE:

gives the single tuple of Fig. 4.7c. There is only one student-name who takes module 2c. If the divisor DDR was the two tuple relation of Fig. 4.7d, then:

DIVIDE DEND BY DDR OVER MODULE

will produce relation 4.7e. Atkins and Johnson both take modules 1 and 1a.

Retrieval requirements may necessitate a combination of operations in order to obtain the desired result. For example, a typical retrieval request may be to find the student names for students who attend any module given by Goodwin. This can be achieved by the following:

SELECT ATTENDANCE WHERE LECTURER-NAME =
'GOODWIN' GIVING TEMP

followed by:

PROJECT TEMP OVER STUDENT-NAME GIVING
RESULT.

The temporary relation TEMP is shown as Fig. 4.8a and RESULT as Fig. 4.8b.

STUDENT-NAME	MODULE
Ashworth	1
Ashworth	1b
Ashworth	2
Ashworth	2a
Ashworth	3
Ashworth	3a
Ashworth	4
Atkins	1
Atkins	1a
Atkins	2
Atkins	2b
Atkins	3
Atkins	3a
Atkins	4
Johnson	1
Johnson	1a
Johnson	2
Johnson	2c
Smith	1
Smith	1b

(a) Dend relation
(part)

DDR

MODULE
2c

(b)

Result

STUDENT-NAME
Johnson

(c)

DDR

MODULE
1
1a

(d)

Result

STUDENT-NAME
Atkins
Johnson

(e)

Fig. 4.7. Results of two divide operations.

Temp

STUDENT-NAME	MODULE	LECTURER-NAME
Ashworth	1b	Goodwin
Atkins	1a	Goodwin
Johnson	1a	Goodwin
Smith	1b	Goodwin

(a) Following SELECT

Result

STUDENT-NAME
Ashworth
Atkins
Johnson
Smith

(b) Following PROJECT

Fig. 4.8. Two-stage retrieval.

To insert a new tuple into the relation, the operator UNION could be used. If, for example, 'Zed' was the name of a new student in the first year, then we might add him to the STUDENT relation by:

STUDENT UNION ('ZED', '1') GIVING STUDENT

and to delete a student:

STUDENT MINUS ('ATKINS', '1') GIVING STUDENT

These procedures are rather awkward and most languages based on the relational algebra 'cheat' and have an ADD and DELETE operator.

The relational algebra is fairly simple and powerful. One criticism, particularly when compared to the relational calculus, is that it is procedural and the user will need some programming experience to be able to formulate a particular request. Many requests may be very involved, with a number of individual statements. For this reason, it should not be looked on as an end user language.

The Relational Calculus

When compared to the relational algebra, the relational calculus is more oriented towards expressing the user requests in a way that the user may construct, because it is non-procedural. This means that the user specifies his needs rather than having to construct the procedures to retrieve the required data. 'Pure' relational calculus is difficult for non-mathematicians, but more user-oriented languages which are based on the relational calculus are easier to use. Codd's Data Sub Language called DSL ALPHA has the general retrieval format:

GET INTO workspace (target list) option list

where, workspace is the name of the area where the retrieved data is to be put; target list gives details of the relation; and option list gives the particular restrictions on the target list. In some implementations of the relational calculus, GET INTO is replaced by RETRIEVE. An example will make this easier to understand:

GET INTO W (ATTENDANCE,STUDENT-NAME)
WHERE (LECTURER-NAME='CLARKE')

Here we are putting into the workspace 'W' the student names of students held in the relation called 'ATTENDANCE' who are taught by the lecturer called 'CLARKE' (see Fig. 4.2). The result in W will be:

STUDENT-NAME
Ashworth
Atkins
Johnson
Smith

The option list can contain < or > (for less than or greater than) as well as = (for equal to).

If a particular relation is frequently referred to in a particular run, then the use of the 'RANGE' statement can reduce the work of the user. For example:

RANGE ATTENDANCE A and

RANGE LECTURER-MODULE L

will allow the user to specify the ATTENDANCE relation using 'A' and LECTURER-MODULE using 'L' as abbreviations. For example:

GET INTO W (L.MODULE) WHERE (L.NO-OF-WEEKS>10)

will give:

MODULE
4

(Module 4 is the only module which lasts longer than 10 weeks.)

It is possible to search through many relations, indeed the whole data base, and the RANGE command can be used to restrict such access by only allowing users to refer to relations defined in a RANGE statement.

DSL ALPHA was specified as a host language system. This means that the programs could be written in Cobol (the host language) and when data is to be retrieved from the data base, the special DSL ALPHA commands will apply. QUEL, the query language for Ingres (see section 7.5), is a user language similar to DSL ALPHA, though it is not a host language system, but a self-contained query language.

SEQUEL (Structured English QUEry Language), sometimes abbreviated to SQL, is a calculus-based language whose basic operation is the mapping of:

SELECT/FROM/WHERE

so that a request:

LIST PARTS ISSUED IN 1985

would be formulated as:

SELECT	PART NAME, QUANTITY	(data items)
FROM	PARTSFILE	(a relation)
WHERE	YEAR=1985.	(qualifiers)

The qualifications on the data retrieved can include ANDs and ORs. As with QUEL (discussed in chapter 7 in the context of Ingres), the user has to know the names of the relevant attributes and key them in explicitly. The user has also to construct a path through the relations thus setting up the linkages required. SQL also provides a CREATE VIEW command which sets up alternative views of the data derived from other tables and selected rows and columns. This is useful when setting up different sub-schemas (which adhere to the security and privacy requirements defined by the data base administrator).

QBE, proposed by Zloof in 1974 is designed for users with little or no programming experience. This cannot be said of the relational algebra and it is more 'user friendly' than a straight relational calculus language such as QUEL or SQL. The intention is that operations in the QBE language are analogous to the way people would naturally use tables. Further, as the name implies, the user can use an example to specify his query. The user enters the name of the table and the system supplies the attribute names. The system details the attributes that the user has indicated an interest. Alternative systems may be menu-based and these prevent even the necessity of recalling the relation names. This means that minimal training is necessary. However there are severe limitations to retain flexibility unless the data base is not very complex. QBE and SQL are discussed further in section 7.2.

4.3   THE HIERARCHICAL APPROACH

In the hierarchical model the data structures are represented by trees with the top entity referred to as the root (of which there can be only one per hierarchy). Subordinate entities are connected to the root and further subordinates connected to them. These are often referred to as parent/child relationships. Figure 4.9 shows the basic structure.

For every occurrence of the parent (which must be ordered), there can be any number of occurrences (including zero) of the child (which must also be ordered). However, a child will have only one parent. In Fig. 4.9 LECTURERS and SUBJECTS are known as 'siblings' because they are of the same level but of different types. If they were occurrences of the same type, they are usually referred to as 'twins'. The complexity of the model will depend on how the data base administrator interprets the conceptual model. Increasing flexibility in use may lead to increases in complexity and slower access times.

The connections or links are explicit in the hierarchical model. Pointers are used to explicitly relate elements of the model. Trees are normally described using linked lists. There are overheads when defining and manipulating hierarchies, and this is particularly apparent when comparisons are made with the relational approach. This becomes worse when hierarchies are made realistically complex.

Many real-life data structures fit into the hierarchical pattern, however, and they are also readily understood. The speaker at many a company induction course will illustrate his organisation or departmental structure using a hierarchical diagram. Many DBMS, including IMS and System2000, are based on the hierarchical approach. Nevertheless, the approach has been included in this text with reservations. The network approach, which will be discussed in section 4.4 can deal with hierarchies as well as networks (many-to-many relationships), and these structures do occur frequently. For example, a lecturer can teach on a number of courses and a course may use a number of lecturers. This network cannot be expressed by one hierarchy.

It is possible to express many-to-many relationships using the hierarchical model, but only by creating two hierarchies. In Fig. 4.10, (a) shows that one course can be given by a number of lecturers, and (b) illustrates that one lecturer can lecture on a number of courses. These form the many-to-many relationship shown in (c). This means that there is likely to be considerable data duplication when a hierarchical data base is used.

The order of the tree is significant. In Fig 4.9, the fact that LECTURER is placed to the left of SUBJECTS, even though they are on the same level, means that the former will be processed first on any search. In the hierarchical model, each node represents a record type (it is an entity) and each entity occurrence is an occurrence of a record (for example, that for the lecturer D.E. Avison).

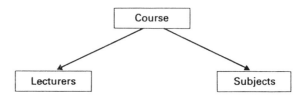

Fig. 4.9. Hierarchy with siblings.

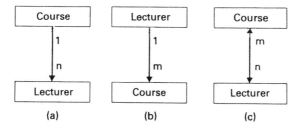

Fig. 4.10. Many-to-many relationships expressed as two hierarchies.

Of course there may be a number of levels in a hierarchy. Figure 4.11 shows such a possibility. Sometimes it is necessary to include intermediate nodes, which do not actually represent records, but are included to maintain the correct hierarchical structure, so that they will be processed in the required order.

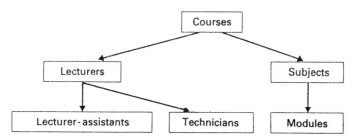

Fig. 4.11. Hierarchy with a number of levels.

The inclusion of SENIOR LECTURERS requires such an intermediate node on the right hand side so as to keep SUBJECTS at the level of LECTURERS who, along with SENIOR LECTURERS, will be responsible for the teaching of the SUBJECTS. This is shown in Fig. 4.12.

When manipulating data in hierarchies, it is necessary to specify to which level a request refers. For example, if the next record is requested, is it the next at that level or at a parent level or at some other level? There is a convention to hierarchical sequence, the ways of visiting trees. The routine is as follows:

VISIT
LEFT and call routine: VISIT
                           LEFT and call routine etc.
                           RIGHT and call routine etc.
RIGHT and call routine   etc.

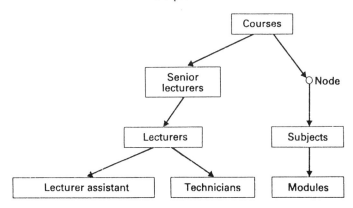

Fig. 4.12. Hierarchy with intermediate node.

The routine will terminate when there are no more branches. It is easiest to understand by following the example given in Fig. 4.13. The sequence here will be A (the root) then left (1), visit B then left (2), visit D, no more left, so back to B (3) and right (4), to visit E, no more left so back to B (5), back to A (6) to right (7) and visit C, back to A (8), no more right and, as it is the root, stop. The dotted lines represent visits to nodes already visited. Thus A, B, D, E and C, is the natural hierarchical sequence in the above hierarchy.

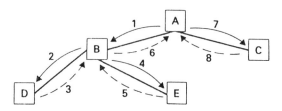

Fig. 4.13. Hierarchical sequence.

Inserting and deleting records also presents a problem. Insertions must be connected to a parent record. Thus to insert a lecturer record, it is necessary to choose a senior lecturer to whom he reports. Deleting a record may also present problems. If the lecturer to be deleted is the only one that reports to a particular senior lecturer, then the information that the senior lecturer did supervise a lecturer is lost if the lecturer record is deleted. One way to avoid losing this information, but perhaps not an ideal solution, is to keep an empty 'lecturer' record for that particular senior lecturer.

The relations developed by data analysis can be readily converted into hierarchies. Each relation is an entity and if a domain is a key in one relation and an attribute or part of a key in another, this would represent a one-to-many hierarchical relationship. Where a many-to-many relationship is implied hierarchies would need to be created for both directions if the model is to represent the 'real world' accurately. In IMS terminology (see section 7.2), the entities are converted to segments, the attributes to fields, and the relationships are represented by hierarchies. Each hierarchy is an IMS 'data base'.

For example, the following two relations, COURSE and SUBJECT both have course as the key, but the latter has it as only part of the composite key with subject. Thus COURSE to SUBJECT represents two record types having a one-to-many relationship.

COURSE   *Course*, Lecturer-in-Charge

SUBJECT   *Course, Subject*, Title, Lecturer, No-of-Hours

In other words, a particular course might have a number of subjects associated with it. The addition of a LECTURER relation:

LECTURER   *Lecturer, Room-no*

and also a LEC-SUBJ relation:

LEC-SUBJ   *Lecturer, Course*, No-of-times-given

would be implying, because Course is also part of the key, that a lecturer can teach a number of courses. This also implies a many-to-many relationship between the hierarchical record types COURSE and LECTURER.

A DDL and a DML for the processing of hierarchies is described in section 7.2, in the context of IMS.

4.4 THE NETWORK APPROACH

As seen in Fig. 4.14, the relationship between COURSES and LECTURERS is a many-to-many relationship and not a hierarchical one. This can be seen in Fig. 4.15. The days of the week in which the lecturer

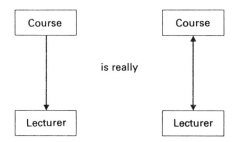

Fig. 4.14. Course-lecturer relationship.

works and gives a course are given in **link records** which need to be set up in these diagrams. Implied in the diagram is that one LECTURER can give more than one COURSE (KL, for example, gives business studies and computer science) and one COURSE is given by a number of LECTURERS (maths by FC and TC, for example) — a many-to-many relationship. Each link record is on two chains which connect the COURSE and LECTURER to it. These link records, sometimes called **connector records**, are usually meaningful in themselves. The link records in the above example could be called CLASS and contain details of the particular class, for example, day, time, room number, and so on.

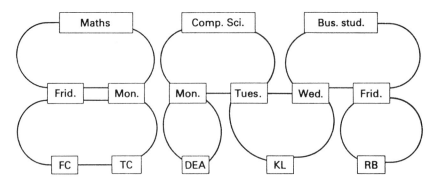

Fig. 4.15. Network with link records.

The occurrences of the records linked together have been represented by pointers. This is a clear way of showing the relationships, but it can be misleading as the linked list with pointers is not the only tool that can be used to link record occurrences. Indeed the means by which record occurrences are related physically is irrelevant to the logical schema. An alternative, data structure diagram technique to relate records, is shown in the case study found in the appendix.

Although the network approach does answer some of the problems of the hierarchical approach, particularly in that it deals with many-to-many relationships, it is more complex. Nevertheless there are a number of DBMS, possibly the most well known being IDMS and Total, which are of this type.

The approach became particularly important after the publication of the Data Base Task Group (DBTG) report of the Codasyl Committee in April 1971. Codasyl (COmmittee of DAta SYstems Languages) originally set up in 1959 is a group of commercial and government computer users in the United States, and representatives from the computer manufacturing world. Its essential purpose is to set up standards for computing which reflect the users' requirements rather than manufacturers' convenience. It was largely responsible for defining the business-oriented Cobol computer language. One of the main uses of computers in commercial data processing is for file and record processing and the DBTG grew out of this concern. The DBTG reports between 1968 and 1981 define a common system for data bases and also feature an analysis of DBMS and distributed data base technology.

One of the main features of the 1971 report is the set concept. If we assume that a LECTURER can only teach one COURSE, and many LECTURERS teach on one COURSE, then the 'closed loop' shown in Fig. 4.16 represents such a set. Each set type is named. This set type is called CLEC. Figure 4.16 (a) is not acceptable from a Codasyl standard, it does not include a set name. Figure 4.16 (b) *is* Codasyl. Set occurrences are shown in Fig. 4.16 (c). The set type has COURSE as the owner record type and LECTURER as the member record type. There can be zero or more occurrences of a member for each occurrence of the owner. Thus a set type can be defined as a named relationship between record types. The latter is a form of an entity, such as COURSE, LECTURER, SUBJECT, and ROOM.

The rules of sets are as follows: a **set** is a collection of named record types and any number of sets can be defined to the data base. A set must have a single owner type. A record type can be a member of one or more sets and can be both owner and member but not of the same set. A set must also have a specified order.

The model can be developed showing more than one level and by having more than one type of record at a particular level, as in Figs 4.17 and 4.18.

One of the problems that the DBTG dealt with was the possibility of having one type of record at a number of levels (described previously as

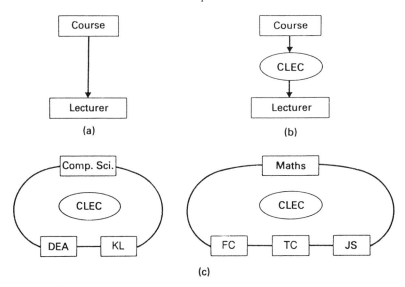

Fig. 4.16. Codasyl sets.

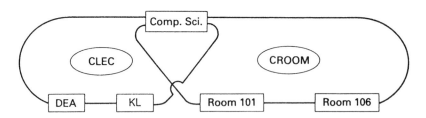

Fig. 4.17. Two set occurrences.

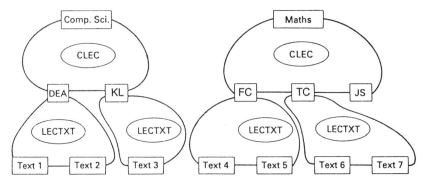

Fig. 4.18. Set occurrences at three levels.

involuted relationships, see Fig. 3.5). Thus a LECTURER could be at a 'head of department', 'course tutor' and 'tutor' level. To cater for this possibility, link records need to be set up. This is shown in Fig. 4.19. As we saw earlier, this technique of setting up link records is used to represent networks. In Fig. 4.20, one COURSE can be given by a number of LECTURES and one LECTURER can give a number of COURSES.

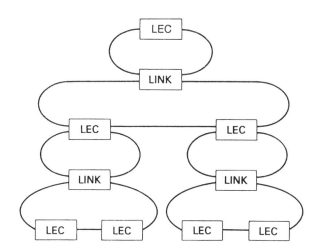

Fig. 4.19. Use of link records — one record type at a number of levels.

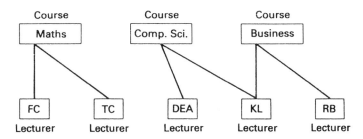

Fig. 4.20. Networks.

The link record is usually not redundant, that is, it contains useful information in itself (in the relational model, it may well have been specified in any case, as a separate relation). In Fig. 4.20, the link records placed between Course and Lecturer could contain data about the day of the week, hours, and room number when the module is presented. This is seen in Fig. 4.15. The course and the lecturer will be used as a composite key which will link the particular course record occurrence and lecturer record occurrence.

Although the network model is more flexible than the hierarchy, the overall structure is fairly complex to implement and requires extra storage space to handle the pointers. As a first approach to converting the conceptual schema to the Codasyl model, the entities become records, attributes to data items, one-to-many relationships to sets, and many-to-many relationships to two sets connected by a link record type.

Languages for Using Networks

The DBTG specification proposed a language for manipulating the files. This data manipulation language (DML) is embodied in a host language. The host language was originally Cobol but other host languages have been specified. The DBTG also specified a language to set up the logical schema, called the data description language (DDL) and a DDL to set up particular user views (sub-schemas) of the data structures. The sub-schema DDL and the DML are extensions to the Cobol language, but even the schema DDL has a Cobol 'flavour', though it is supposed to be language-independent. The sub-schema DDL has to be compatible with Cobol (or the chosen language) as it will be embedded in it.

The DBTG report did not suggest a standard for the **Device and Media Control Language** (DMCL), that is the language controlling the physical access to storage devices, because this would be dependent on the particular hardware used. However the original Codasyl proposals were considered by many to have a "physical schema flavour" as well as presenting a standard for the logical schema. In the later report of 1978, a **Data Storage Description Language** (DSDL) was proposed and this included many of these physical (that is implementation) aspects. It corresponds to a DMCL in part.

The Schema DDL is the language to set up the global data description. The language is distinct and self-contained and it is not dependent on an established programming language. It enables the specification of the various record types (including the individual data items such as Lecturer, Name, and Age in the Lecturer record) and the specification of set types relating these records. It is envisaged in the report that a data base administrator would be responsible for this overall schema data definition and at least oversee the setting up of the user views (via the sub-schema DDL). This was certainly perceptive, and most practitioners would argue strongly for the role of the DBA.

The concept of **areas** which is proposed in the Codasyl report is also an interesting one. Although it is associated with the Schema DDL, it is an important consideration in the physical storage of the data. It is a named portion of accessible storage space in which records are to be stored. It may contain occurrences of records, or sets, or parts of sets. This concept is one of the features of the original report which is open to criticism because it is specifying 'physical' considerations at the logical level (the Schema DDL) and therefore may sacrifice some of the data independence of the model. When assigning records to areas, the DBA has to reconcile a trade-off. On the one hand, increasing the number of areas allows files to be distributed on a number of areas of storage. This will optimise performance and increase integrity and security, so that concurrent access to areas can be prevented. Further, as back-up and restore procedures are carried out by areas, a program with exclusive access to a particular area will not exclude access to other areas. The price to be paid for this is the consequent complexity of the procedures. In view of these considerations, particularly its implementation aspect, it is not surprising that the area concept was removed in the 1979 specification.

The sub-schema DDL allows the setting up of particular user views of part of the schema, such as the specification of privacy locks, and the renaming and redescription of data items and records. Some sub-schemas could overlap.

The data manipulation language represents extensions to the Cobol language specification. This allows data on the data base to be manipulated. It thus includes GET and FIND for reading records on the data base (equivalent to the Cobol READ) and STORE and INSERT which are equivalent to the WRITE statement. ERASE is similar to the Cobol DELETE statement. It removes records from the data base. We will look at these languages in more detail in section 7.3, which discusses IDMS, a Codasyl-orientated DBMS.

4.5 CONCLUSION

Of the three approaches to data base design, relational data bases are possibly the most flexible, as access paths can be defined as and when necessary. Further, there is no need for an experienced programmer or DBA to accomplish the joins and other commands necessary to set up the required queries. However, relational DBMS usually require the user to be aware of the relations that have been set up. The user also needs to know the operations that can be applied to the relations so as to carry out the desired retrievals. Run time performances may also be less good, as the links between relations are set up at run time and not at data definition time. Storage space may also be greater, unless the other systems use a large number of pointers to support data base use.

In the network and hierarchical DBMS the access paths are defined by the DBA before the data base is set up. Although these access paths can be changed at a later date, this can be achieved only with considerable difficulty. It will probably necessitate reorganising part of the data base. Relational data bases do not have this problem. The hierarchical data base only allows downward access paths, and a member at one level cannot be an owner of a record at a higher level. The network system allows access paths to be defined at any level and thus allows much greater flexibility. However, in assessing DBMS there are other factors to bear in mind, and, in any case, not all DBMS of each 'type' follow the ideal, and some have taken steps to correct many of the disadvantages of the type.

REFERENCES

Codasyl Systems Committee (1971) *Feature Analysis of Generalised Database Management Systems.* ACM, New York.
> Gives a basis on which to compare DBMS.
Codasyl Programming Languages Committee (DBTG) (1971) Report, BCS and ACM.
Codasyl Data Description Language Committee (1978) *DDL Journal of Development.*
> These two publications of Codasyl (and others) define the standard. The latter publication contains an appendix relating to the Data Storage Description Language.
Codd, E.F. (1972) 'Relational Completeness of Data Base Sublanguages', in *Data Base Systems.* Courant Computer Science Symposia Series, Vol. 6. Prentice Hall, Englewood Cliffs, NJ.
> Gives a formal definition of the relational algebra and calculus.
Date, C.J. (1981) *An Introduction to Database Systems,*3rd edn. Addison Wesley, Cambridge, Mass.
> A very thorough analysis of the subject and contains a very good description of the three types of logical schema and their associated data definition and data manipulation languages.
Zloof, M.M. (1977) 'Query by Example: A Data Base Language', *IBM Systems Journal,* **16,** 4.

Chapter 5

The Physical Schema
File Access and Organisation

5.1 ORGANISATION OF DATA ON BACKING STORAGE MEDIA

The **physical schema** represents the various file organisation methods that are supported by computer systems. It is sometimes referred to as the **internal schema**. File organisation refers to the way that the records have been structured on disk, thus it refers to the record storage and how the records are linked together. File access refers to the way that the records can be retrieved for the purpose of reading the data, changing it, adding to it and deleting it. In common with most texts, this uses file organisation to mean both the data storage structure and access.

Serial files are the simplest form of file organisation. The records are not stored in any particular sequence apart from that of first in, first out. This is simple to create, but makes the retrieval of any particular record slow as the file has to be searched until the required record is found. Because data base systems require fast retrieval, this method of organising data is unlikely to be appropriate.

A second method of file organisation is to store records in a particular sequence. A file of lecturers may be stored in lecturer number or lecturer name sequence. The records need to be sorted in order of a particular (key) field before storing the data on to the file. **Sequential** files are easy to use, they will support records of variable length and they use the backing storage media space efficiently. Sequential organisation has the major advantage that the records are stored in a logical order, presumably that sequence to which the records are normally required for printing and for soft copy reports. However, sequential ordering still does not cater for the particular requirements of most data base uses. As Fig. 5.1 shows, records cannot be inserted into the file without rewriting that file. Further, particular records cannot be searched for directly. A search has still to be carried out of the file until the particular record required is found. Tape files can only be accessed in this way and therefore they can only support serial or sequential files.

If the file is stored on disc, however, there are possible answers to

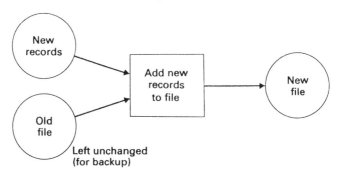

Fig. 5.1. Adding new records to a sequential file.

the problem. One solution would be to store an **index** (Fig. 5.2). This will contain the key alongside the address where the record is stored. The record address can be retrieved following an index 'look-up' operation. With the address, the record can be located. This address could be an actual physical address or some sort of relative address: relative, that is, to the beginning of the file.

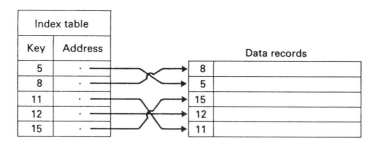

Fig. 5.2. Indexed files.

The process of (a) searching the index to find the address of the required record, and (b) going directly to that address, will be considerably faster than searching through all the records on a sequential file.

Sometimes the index is sorted, making access quicker, particularly when using the **binary chop** method of searching. Here, the key of the record to be accessed is compared to the key of the middle record on the index. If the desired key is higher than this, the key is compared to the third quartile record (if lower, to the first quartile record). The process continues until the matching key is found. Figure 5.3 shows the method. Four searches of the index table are required in order to find the address of record 30. Serial searching will take eleven accesses of the index.

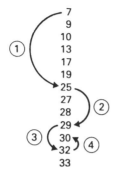

Fig. 5.3. Binary search (or 'binary chop').

The **indexed sequential** method of file organisation which is common on conventional files may be appropriate for some data base uses. This is based on a combination of the sequential and the index files described earlier. The file is created in sequential order of a key field. It can therefore be processed sequentially. An index is created at the same time. Unlike the non-sequential indexed file discussed previously, an index to every record need not be held. Instead there is a reference to only one record for each block of data. The key of this record will be the highest in that block, which usually corresponds to a track on a disk.

Figure 5.4 shows a file of three blocks of data. The index contains the keys of the records ending each block along with the address of the beginning of that block. If the key requested is 24, then the index table will be searched to see in which block it is to be found. The address of the beginning of the relevant (third) block can then be found, located, and searched through sequentially until the required record is located. Thus index sequential files, even when processed by key, do not eliminate sequential processing, but it limits it to one block. Frequently a cylinder index is added as a first level index. The particular track index can then be located. Even then, if a file is very large, it may spread over a number of disks. In that case there will be a further preliminary search through a disk index.

Access speeds may still be slow for many purposes in a data base environment. Updating and deleting are straightforward. The record is accessed (as previously described), changed or deleted (or marked 'for deletion'). An addition to the indexed sequential file can present difficulties. Indeed it will require complete reorganisation of the file unless precautions are taken for the records should be retained in sequential order to permit sequential access. One usual method is to leave gaps at

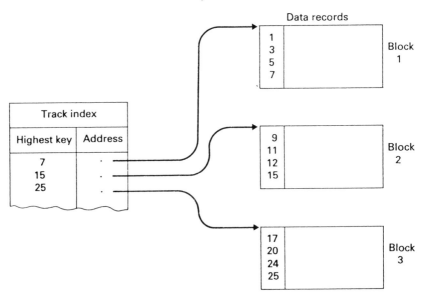

Fig. 5.4. Index sequential file.

the end of each block so that records can be inserted into a block (with only slight reorganisation of the records in that block to maintain the correct order). Figure 5.5 illustrates how a record with key number 5 can be inserted.

1	
4	
7	
—	
—	

1	
4	
5	
7	
—	

Fig. 5.5. Index sequential files — record insertion.

Another possible way of allowing for addition is to set up a special block, called the **overflow block** (see Fig. 5.6). When a data block overflows, a pointer will be maintained to point to the address of the overflow block. Eventually reorganisation of the complete file is necessary to avoid poor performance.

A true **direct access** file is one where there is a direct relationship between the key field of a record and a unique address on disk. Processing is therefore minimal and the records will be stored in sequence.

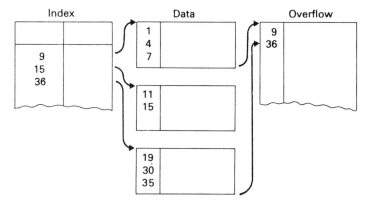

Fig. 5.6. Index sequential files — overflow block.

Keys have to be numeric and space has to be reserved on disk to hold records of every key that can possibly exist in the defined range. If many keys do not have records associated with them, then there is wastage in storage space. Indeed, few files seem in practice to conform to this requirement. Random access is more usual, and these files are often called (mistakenly) direct access files.

Random access (sometimes known as **indirect addressing**) offers another way of organising data on disk for quick access. The DBMS allocates space on disk and a record is allocated to a particular slot via a randomising (or 'hashing') algorithm which is designed to use the allocated space efficiently. The **randomising algorithm** translates the key of the record to a physical address on disk and the system places the record there. The formula will not produce files in sequential order. If the space is already being utilised by another record, then the record that is presently being processed is placed in either the next available space or in an overflow area allocated for that purpose. There is a wide range of possible algorithms. The designer has to choose one which is appropriate for the file.

Random access files can present problems. Their advantage lies in the speed of accessing a particular record as the randomising formula converts the key of a record to an address on disk. But a good randomising formula is often difficult to construct because a 'good' formula will depend on the area on disk available and the particular spread of keys. By 'good' we mean that the area on disk allocated for the file is well used — very critical for large files. This is referred to as a high **packing density**. It is also important that there are not many **synonyms**. A synonym occurs when the application of the randomising formula to two or more keys gives the same address. In this case, most systems look for the next available space when storing the data. If this occurs frequently, it can greatly slow down access speeds and lead to the loss of speed of the system, and therefore the advantage of random access is also lost.

The file organisation methods so far discussed do not respond to all the desired features of data base systems. In particular, a data base user may want to search a file in a number of ways, according to a particular application. A file of lecturers, for example, may be searched for according to lecturer number, lecturer name, status, or qualification. A possible solution, but one which contains considerable data duplication, would be to store the files in a number of ways. In other words to have a file of lecturers in lecturer number order, another in status order, and another in name order. Sorting records for each application would also be too slow. This solution would be very inefficient in storage space and, if data changed, it would be necessary to update a number of files.

Assuming that the DBMS permits a number of alternative file organisation techniques, the actual organisation chosen for any particular data structure will depend on which is the most efficient for that particular application and this decision will be made by the data base administrator. The file organisation method chosen could even be serial or sequential, particularly if the data is likely to be accessed in batch mode. Most DBMS can process data both in real-time and batch mode. If the use of the data changes, then its organisation should be capable of being changed without the users being aware of it (known as **physical data independence**), apart, that is, from the gains in speed. The systems of file organisation most suited to data base management systems are the various forms of list organisation and inverted file. These are discussed in the following sections.

5.2 LISTS

One of the obvious ways of organising the data on physical storage media is by using lists. In fact the Codasyl DBTG started life as the List Processing Task Group but changed its name on investigating the wider issues of their task. A list structure joins a sequence of data elements by including along with each data element a pointer, which is itself a field, relating to the next data element in the list. This pointer could refer to the actual address, for example, the cylinder, track and head number on a disk. Usually it refers to a relative address, the location of the next record when compared to the address of the record being presently processed. Alternatively, it may be a symbolic address, which is converted to an actual address via some form of key transformation scheme. This logical identifier has to uniquely identify the record and its actual address can also be obtained by looking up a table containing the addresses of all the identifiers.

Figure 5.7 (a) shows a list of lecturers with details completed in Fig. 5.7 (b). The full stop represents a pointer to the address of the next record in the list. The word 'null' marks the end of the list. Obviously much of the data relating to each lecturer (such as department, salary, address, telephone number, courses taught) has been omitted. These records need not be held in this 'logical' sequence (see Fig. 5.7c), as long as the files are held on direct access storage devices. One of the advantages of list processing is that data can be processed sequentially without the records being stored sequentially.

Records are added by changing the pointer references (see Fig. 5.7d). If Fred Bloggs of number 5136 was added to the list then the pointer contained in D. Avison should be changed to point to 5136 (and not to 5138) and the pointer in Bloggs should contain 5138. This maintains the required sequence. Deletion requires a similar exercise.

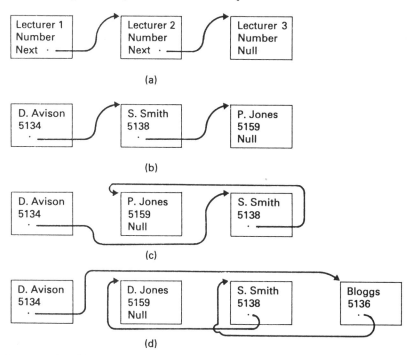

Fig. 5.7. Linked lists.

To facilitate easier access it may also be necessary to add other pointers (Fig. 5.8) such as a pointer to the beginning of the list or to the previous record as well as the next one. It may be convenient to point to the first record in that list, in which case the list is a **circular list**, **ring** or **chain** (see Fig.5.9).

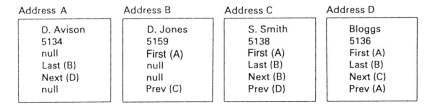

Address A	Address B	Address C	Address D
D. Avison	D. Jones	S. Smith	Bloggs
5134	5159	5138	5136
null	First (A)	First (A)	First (A)
Last (B)	null	Last (B)	Last (B)
Next (D)	null	Next (B)	Next (C)
null	Prev (C)	Prev (D)	Prev (A)

Fig. 5.8. Records with a number of pointers.

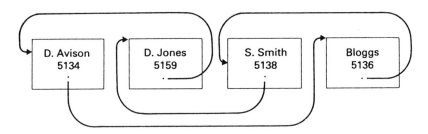

Fig. 5.9. Circular lists.

For most DBMS applications, the lists required will be more complex. For one thing, there is likely to be various levels in the structure. This will support the tree structures (Fig. 5.10) that data bases frequently are required to represent. DBMS are therefore expected to support multiple linked lists if they adopt the list processing method of file organisation.

Tree structures can be balanced or unbalanced. Each node in the former will have the same number of children. Binary trees are balanced, each node having two children and two pointers. This can result in fast access if the application files lend themselves to this type of structure.

To implement a network, it is necessary to have a series of pointers at each record occurrence. A realistic example would therefore have a considerable overhead in space for pointers and, more importantly,

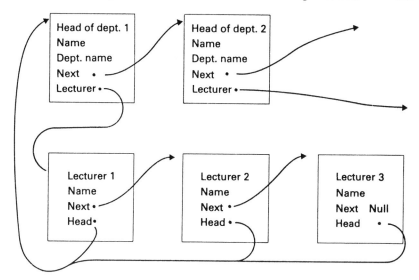

Fig. 5.10. List processing — tree structures.

time to access a record through a list may be slow. The example in Fig. 5.10 could support a network. Both the department head lists will hold the same pointers downward as the lecturers hold upwards, that is, all types of access between the two 'levels' is permitted.

The various records are likely to contain more data. The lecturer records might contain the age, qualifications, years of experience, salary, and so on. The list structure allows other fields within records to be linked (though this flexibility may be paid for in terms of complexity and other overheads). There may, for instance, be a requirement to join together lecturers of a similar qualification or age group.

In Fig. 5.11 there is one list of four records joining the lecturers together. There are also three lists joining lecturers within similar age groups. The first of these (less than 10 years) has only one record, J.Smith. The second list joins two records, that of D.Avison and T.Jones, who have less than 20 years experience. The final list (over 20 years experience) contains only the one record, that of T.Davis.

Frequently there will be other pointers. In a hierarchy, a pointer is likely to refer to the owner record — on each lecturer record there could be a pointer to its owner, the head of department. This would be useful to support quick processing of enquiries.

The negative aspect of providing this flexibility is the added complexity, in particular to support insertions, deletions and updates. Poin-

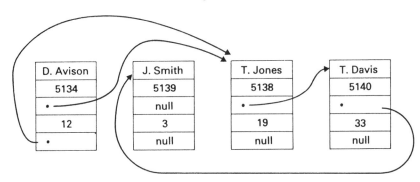

Fig. 5.11. Records with a number of lists.

ters have to be maintained for each of these operations, so time will be spent maintaining pointers as much as updating data. Furthermore, the software to support this requirement will also be fairly complex. It is essential that links are not lost when maintaining pointers. The data base administrator has to think very carefully when setting up numerous lists as to whether their use will justify their overheads.

5.3 INVERTED FILES

In some applications the list structure has serious drawbacks. One type of enquiry which is slow in list processing and inverted files deal with much more efficiently is illustrated by the example: 'Is there a lecturer with a name Perkins on the staff?'. In a list file, this requires access to all records on the 'lecturer name' list until the Perkins occurrence is found. This simple enquiry, which a user may 'feel' ought to have an immediate response might take some seconds to process.

With inverted files the records are held in a data area on disk, but there is also an index which contains values or a range of values for some of the data. These will be the nominated key fields. Along with these are associated pointers containing the addresses of the record(s) with those corresponding field values. Normally the pointers are relative, rather than actual, addresses. This allows for changes of physical location without changing the index, thus providing some level of data independence. Another possible gain in efficiency is to hold the indexes of the inverted file in sequential order so that the binary search (discussed in section 5.1) can be applied.

Many queries can be answered by simply accessing the index. Fields which may be frequently accessed may be designated key fields by the data base administrator and held on the index, to facilitate this easy access. There are overheads in storing these indexes and this factor needs to be weighed with ease of access. Record insertion, deletion and update involve high costs. Large files will have a number of inverted indexes. Sometimes there is an overall key index and pointers to the relative addresses of the particular key indexes required to be searched. A further possibility is to combine the list and inverted file. The inverted file will have an index which points to lists of certain types of record.

There may be a number of data items in a record that are chosen to be indexed. In Fig. 5.12, a lecturer's qualification and department are indexed but not name or date of birth. Of course there is a price to pay. The 'ideal' 100% inversion, where all data items are keys, and therefore all items are contained in an index as well as a data record, will be very inefficient in many respects. When deleting a record, not only has the data record to be deleted but all mentions of it in the indexes have also to be deleted. For additions, the record is created and the index must include references to it where appropriate. When updating, care has to be exercised when the field updated is one which is indexed.

Index			Data records	
Key name	Key value	Address	Address	Data
Qual.	B.A.	50	40	J. Smith
		80		Ph.D.
	M.Sc.	60		Comp. Sci.
	Ph.D	40		1947
Dept.	Comp. Sci.	40	60	T. Davis
		80		M.Sc.
	Maths	60		Maths
	Business	50		1961
			80	R. Jones
				B.A.
				Comp. Sci.
				1954
			50	T. Hanes
				B.A.
				Business
				1945

Fig. 5.12. Inverted file.

Yet there are considerable advantages of such an approach. Queries of the type 'Are there?' or 'How many?' become simple if the information is held in the index. For example: 'Do any lecturers have a Ph.D?'

or 'How many lecturers are in the Computer Science Department?' can be answered by accessing the index only. If there are expected to be a number of queries of the type 'How many lecturers are over 40 years of age?', the data base administrator may well consider using date-of-birth as a key for inclusion in the index. More complex queries requiring 'and' and/or 'or' can be described such as 'Is there a lecturer who has a Ph.D. and is in the Business Department?'. The answer can be obtained by access to the index only.

When there are a large number of keys, it may be convenient to have a secondary index as shown in Fig. 5.13.

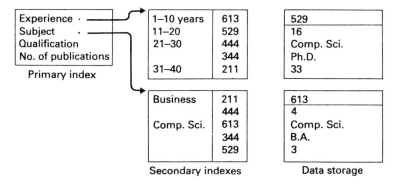

Fig. 5.13. Use of secondary indexes.

5.4 CONCLUSION

If the data base administrator has the choice of file organisation then that chosen will depend on the application. Some data base management systems support a number of file organisation methods and many will help the data base administrator by simulating the requirements of the application on various file organisation types. Some only support one file organisation technique.

REFERENCES

Dodd, G.C. (1969) 'Elements of Data Management Systems', *Computing Surveys*, (June 1969).
Provides a clear, concise account of the various ways of file organisation and access.

Knuth, D.E. (1973) *The Art of Computer Programming,* Vol. 1, *Fundamental Algorithms,* 2nd edn (1973), and Vol. 3, *Sorting and Searching* (1973). Addison-Wesley, Reading, Mass.

Martin, J. (1977) *Computer Data-Base Organization*, 2nd edn. Prentice Hall, Englewood Cliffs, N.J.

Chapter 6

Implementing Application Systems

6.1 CONVENTIONAL SYSTEMS ANALYSIS

Once the data base, or at least the relevant part, has been set up, applications can be implemented which use it. Some applications will require the user to use the query language of the DBMS. Typically, a sales manager may make enquiries of the data base of the type: 'Which customers have exceeded their credit status?' or 'Which products have not reached their sales targets?'. Alternatively the sales manager may request a listing of sales figures to be produced by the DBMS report writer. Most DBMS query languages and report generators are very adept at dealing with these requests without difficulty.

In a data base environment, many applications are large operational systems, such as sales order processing, sales ledger, production control, stock control, and invoicing. These systems have to be designed and implemented and they could be run daily or weekly for some years without many major alterations. They will usually be written in conventional programming languages such as Cobol or PL/1 and not use the query language provided with the DBMS.

In section 1.2 some critical comments were made of conventional systems analysis. Some of these criticisms applied because of their file orientation. This type of criticism should not apply in a data base environment. Here there should be a separation of data aspects from processing aspects. Sets of data which may be required in a number of applications need not be collected more than once. The data will be shared on the data base. Further, modifications in systems are likely to be much easier to make, because files are external to the program. Changes to the data may only involve changing the relevant parts of the data base, and the many programs that may use the data will not need to be changed.

But there are a number of good points associated with the conventional approach. The six stages (feasibility study, systems investigation, systems analysis, systems design, implementation, and review and maintenance) associated with conventional systems analysis have been well tried and tested. At the end of each stage the analyst and manage-

126

ment have an opportunity to review progress in the development of the application. There are a number of documentation aids which aids the analysis, design and implementation processes, particularly in helping to ensure that the work is thorough and can be communicated to interested parties.

Another argument in its support is that many of the developments in systems analysis such as structured systems analysis, participation and prototyping which are discussed later in this chapter can be incorporated into the conventional approach. This can make the conventional approach perfectly adequate for some systems development work.

But as we saw in section 1.3, there are serious limitations to the conventional approach. There is a danger that the new system merely 'computerises' the clerical system used previously. Frequently it is designed quickly in order to solve a problem that has occurred with the old system. A 'quick and dirty' solution may be politically expedient but may well cause considerable problems, particularly with regard to the maintenance workload. The new design is therefore likely to be unambitious, may not be tested properly, and is unlikely to take full account of the potential of the technology used. The conventional methodology tends to pay lip service to user involvement. There is no mechanism to enforce user involvement and it is therefore often ignored. This frequently results in the system being rejected by the users.

This rejection of the system may be a result of poor analysis: the systems analyst has not found out the user requirements. The user may not have been involved to the extent of being able to see the repercussions of the system design he had 'agreed' with the analyst. The documentation provided is oriented towards computer people and it is difficult for users to translate many of these forms used in conventional systems documentation into their 'language'. If systems are developed without the involvement of the users, they may be unwilling to accept the new systems because they feel it has been imposed on them. Systems may therefore be rejected as soon as they are implemented.

The data base approach is long term and costly, and therefore top management should not risk its failure by sticking to outdated methods of applications development. The failure of one application could jeapordise all applications. For this reason it is essential to pay regard to changes in techniques of applications development. Participation and prototyping could be used independently in some applications and in others it may be appropriate to use the conventional approach modified by incorporating these tools and techniques.

6.2   STRUCTURED SYSTEMS ANALYSIS AND DESIGN

The term 'structured' is very fashionable in computing. It has been adopted by many authors and consultants and it seems to mean many things, depending on the author and context. The essential feature of structured techniques is the breaking down of a complex problem into smaller manageable units in a systematic (disciplined) way. The techniques use a number of pictorial methods of presenting results and these can be understood by users and analysts alike.

Structured techniques are relevant to systems analysis *and* design. Systems analysis could be described as 'what is' and 'what is required' whilst systems design is 'what could be'. Using the technique of **functional decomposition**, a very complex problem can be broken down into a number of fairly complex parts and then further to less complex parts until, at the bottom level, all the parts are fairly trivial and therefore easy to understand.

As can be seen in Fig. 6.1, 'produce weekly payroll' at the top level can be broken into 'validate weekly return', 'calculate gross wage', 'calculate deductions' and 'print wages slip'. Each of these boxes is separate and, when at the program level, can be altered without affecting the other boxes. Each of these steps can be further broken down, a process also referred to as **stepwise refinement**. For example, 'calculate deductions' can be broken down into 'calculate tax', 'calculate national insurance contribution', and 'calculate loan repayments'. Eventually this 'top down' approach can lead to the level of a few simple English statements or a small amount of programming code.

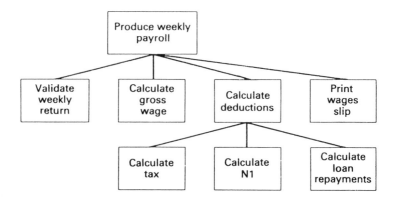

Fig. 6.1. Functional decomposition.

This technique has had a great deal of impact in computer programming where it has led to more reliable programs which are easier to maintain, and it is likely to be at least as important in systems analysis and design. Books by Gane and Sarson (1979) and DeMarco (1979), and others have had considerable impact. To some extent these books propagate a series of techniques. The techniques include data flow diagrams, data structure diagrams, decision trees, decision tables, and structured English. These techniques are a great improvement on more established techniques, such as flowcharting, which typify conventional systems analysis. Most of these newer techniques of systems analysis and design have in fact been with us for some time, but were not brought together until the late 1970s.

These techniques prove to be a considerable improvement on those of conventional systems analysis, both from the point of view of understanding the real-world processes that they represent, and in communicating the knowledge acquired. Structured analysis documentation includes documents describing the logical (real-world) analysis of the processes and not just their physical (implementation) level designs. In other words, there is a clear distinction between any application logic and the computer representation of that logic. There will be a separation of any data or information that the system is likely to want to input, output, process, or store, and the physical record, that is the computer file or part of a data base. The analysis documentation will include a system's inputs, outputs and data structures as well as the processing logic.

Data Flow Diagrams (DFD) are a particularly useful aid in communicating the analyst's understanding of the system. They do so by partitioning the system into independent units of a size that enable the system to be easily understood. The user, whether the operator of the system when it is operational or the manager of the department it is aimed to help, can readily check that the DFD is accurate because it is so graphical. DFDs can be converted into computer procedures.

There are four parts to the DFD. This is standard, though there are a number of different graphical conventions in showing them. The convention used here is suggested by Gane and Sarson. The arrow represents a data flow from one part of the system to another. In Fig. 6.2 an example of a data flow is the delivery notes passing from one supplier to the process 'check notes against order'. A second part of the diagram is represented by 'bubbles' or rounded boxes which are used to denote processes. A third element is the data store, such as the store of purchase orders in Fig. 6.2.

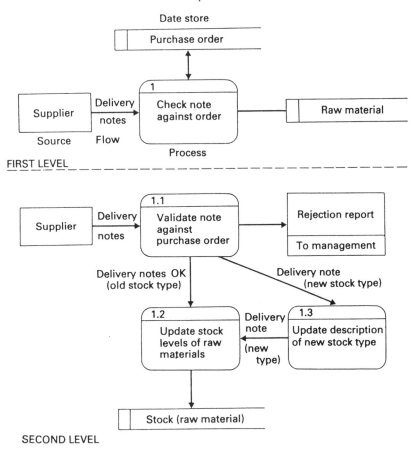

Fig. 6.2. Data flow diagrams — top level and more detailed second level.

A fourth part of data flow diagrams are 'sources' and 'sinks', usually external, such as a customer, a supplier or the Inland Revenue. We are not interested in them as such (they are outside the boundary of the investigation), but we are interested in what they give. For example, it is not the customers themselves which are important, but their orders. Similarly it is not the warehouse that is important, but the drain on stock. These are represented by boxes. One of the main features of data flow diagrams is the ability to construct them in levels each reflecting greater detail (reflecting functional decomposition of the process). For example, the process contained in a soft box in one level could be a whole DFD in another. This is illustrated in Fig. 6.2. Note that the process numbered 1 in the top part of the diagram is represented by 1.1, 1.2, and 1.3 in the more detailed version below.

Data flow diagrams prove to be a good communication tool and only the major features of systems are drawn to help clarity. In drawing a data flow diagram, the analyst will start by drawing a 'doodle' attempt of the whole system, and a number of lower level 'doodles'. These are then refined iteratively to the analyst's satisfaction. This version is then presented to the users for their comment. Further iterations of the diagram are therefore likely before the final versions are produced.

Structured English, decision trees and decision tables are alternative methods of describing process logic. They are appropriate in different circumstances but each provides simple, clear, and unambiguous ways of describing the logic of what happens in a particular process. Natural language is ambiguous and long-winded and these techniques are much superior.

Structured English, for example, is very like a 'readable' computer program. It is not a programming language though it can be readily converted to a computer program, because it is a strict and logical form of English and the constructs reflect structured programming. Structured English is a precise way of specifying a function and is readily understandable by the systems designer as well as being readily converted to a program. An example is given in Fig. 1.12. Structured English uses only a limited subset of English and this vocabulary is exact. This ensures less ambiguity in the use of 'English' by the analyst. Further, by the use of text indentation, the logic of the process can be shown easier.

Structured English has an:

    IF condition 1 (is true)
        THEN action 2 (is to be carried out)
    ELSE (not condition 1)
        SO action 1 (to be carried out)

construct. Conditions can include equal, not equal, greater than, less than, and so on. There are alternative languages such as 'Pseudo Code', and 'Tight English'. These vary on their nearness to the machine or readability to users.

A **decision tree** illustrates the actions to be taken at each decision point. The actions follow each decision point via a branch of a tree whereas each condition will determine the particular branch to be followed. The techniques of showing decisions and actions are graphical and easy to understand unless it becomes so large that it is difficult to follow. An example of a decision tree is given in Fig. 6.3. They are constructed by first identifying the conditions, actions, unless/however/ but structures from narrative. Each sentence may form a mini decision tree and these will be joined together to form the version which will be verified by the users. Decision trees prove to be a good method of showing the basics of a decision, that is, what are the possible actions that might be taken at a particular decision point and what set of values leads to each of these actions. It is easy for the user to verify whether the analyst has understood the procedures.

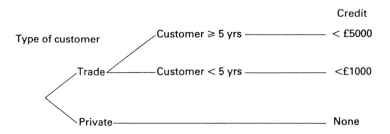

Fig. 6.3. Decision tree.

Decision tables are less graphical but are concise and have an in-built verification mechanism so that it is possible to check that all the conditions have been catered for. An example of a decision table is shown as Fig. 6.4. Decision tables can be used as computer input, programs being produced directly from them, and there are a number of packages available for this purpose.

Figure 6.4 shows the decisions that have to be made by drivers in the U.K. at traffic lights. The table has four sections. The condition stub has the possible conditions 'red', 'amber' and 'green'. Condition Entries are either Y for yes (this condition is satisfied) or N for no (this condition is not satisfied. Having three conditions, there will be 2 to the power of 3 ($2\times2\times2 = 8$) columns. The easiest way of proceding is to have the first row as YYYYNNNN, the second row as YYNNYYNN and the final row as YNYNYNYN. If there were four conditions, we would start by eight Ys and eight Ns and so on.

All the possible actions are listed in the Action Stub. An X placed on a row/column coincidence in the Action Entry means that the action in the condition stub should be taken. A blank will mean that the action should not be taken. Thus, if a driver is faced with Red (Y), Amber (Y)

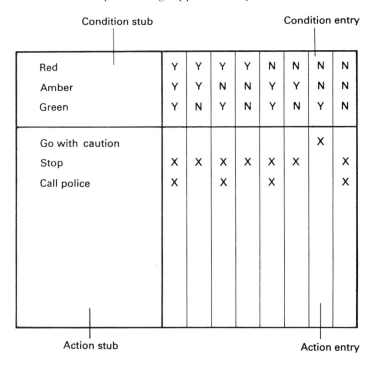

Condition stub   Condition entry

Red	Y	Y	Y	Y	N	N	N	N
Amber	Y	Y	N	N	Y	Y	N	N
Green	Y	N	Y	N	Y	N	Y	N
Go with caution							X	
Stop	X	X	X	X	X	X		X
Call police	X		X		X			X

Action stub   Action entry

Fig. 6.4. Decision table.

and Green (Y), the first column indicates that the driver should stop and call the police. All combinations, even invalid ones, should be considered. The next column Red (Y), Amber (Y) and Green (N) informs the driver to stop. Only the Red (N), Amber (N) and Green (Y) combination permits the driver to go with caution.

In systems analysis, there are likely to be requirements to specify actions where there are a large number of conditions. A set of decision tables is appropriate here. The first will have actions such as 'GO TO Decision Table 2' or to GO TO DT3. Each of these may themselves be reduced to a further level of decision tables. The technique lends itself to functional decomposition.

Structured methodologies use techniques which can be followed by analysts and users alike and, therefore, pay attention to the 'people side of systems'. In the past, systems analysts were first and foremost computer people. Now at least they are talking a language that the rest of the organisation can understand. This is important in getting the willing participation of users. Most of the documentation aids are graphic representations of the subject matter. This is much easier to follow than text which is long-winded and frequently ambiguous or file designs or programming flowcharts which are understandable only to the computer professional.

Gane and Sarson and other writers on structured analysis also advocate the use of data dictionaries (discussed in chapter 9 of this text) and other tools of data analysis, such as normalisation, as part of the methodology. Forms for detailing the data elements and data stores are also provided. In this text, we have attempted to separate these data-oriented aspects, particularly data analysis and data bases, from the process-oriented aspects. In practise, the distinction is never clear-cut.

As well as improved communication tools, the methodology usually incorporates **structured walkthroughs**. These are team meetings where the analysis and design specifications and other documentation are exposed to review by the members of the team. It is usual that they represent meetings of peers and that 'management' are not involved. This is to avoid the type of criticism which may have repercussions later on the team member's status or salary. A peer review is likely to reveal errors, omissions, ambiguities, and weaknesses in style and also help to motivate and train the staff involved.

Questions that the peer group are likely to as of a design could include:

(1) Can bespoke programs use library routines?

(2) Is the user interface simple, understandable, consistent?

(3) Does the design fulfil the specification fully?

(4) Will it work?

Structured walkthroughs should avoid the late detection of errors and flaws in logic and hence greatly reduce the risk of failure when the system is running.

Structured systems analysis and design need not only be seen as an alternative to the conventional approach. The different authors of the approach do not view structured analysis in the same way. Some regard the techniques as a useful alternative to many techniques of the conventional approach and therefore should be incorporated in the conventional approach. Other writers, for example Gane and Sarson, emphasise a 'structured methodology' which should replace the conventional approach. DeMarco regards these techniques to be in the realm of analysis only and considers design to be a separate process where the analyst uses his experience and imagination to 'invent' a new system. Gane and Sarson suggest that the techniques can be used to specify the system design and aid implementation. They discuss query types and their implication for physical factors. They also ask users to construct a 'wish list' defining their requirements and providing a menu of alternatives. Writers also emphasise different techniques, although some techniques are common to all. It is functional decomposition which really separates the structured systems approach from other approaches.

6.3 PARTICIPATION

This is a practical philosophy aimed at providing solutions to user problems. The belief here is that people have a basic right to control their own destinies and that, if they are allowed to participate in the analysis and design of the system that they will be using, then the implementation, acceptance and operation of the systems that they will be using will be enhanced.

In the conventional systems analysis methodology, the importance of user involvement is frequently stressed although it is not 'built in' to the methodology as are, for example, the various documentation requirements. However the computer person is the person who is making the real decisions. In practice participation may mean (a) 'doing a public relations job to placate the staff' and (b) 'Once that is done train them to use the system'. This is not what we mean by participation. Systems analysts are trained in and knowledgable of the technological and economic aspects of computer applications but far more rarely on the human aspects which are at least as important. The person who is going to use the system, frequently feels resentment and top management frequently does little more than pay lip-service to computing.

When the system is implemented, the systems analyst may be happy with the system. This is of little significance if the users are not happy with it. They are the customers. Many systems may 'work' in that they are technically viable, but fail because of 'people problems'. Users may feel that the new system will make their job less secure, will make their relationship with others change for the worse, or will lead to a loss of the independence that they previously enjoyed.

As a result of these feelings, users may do their best to ensure that the computer system will not succeed. This may show itself in attempts to 'beat the system'. Frequently it manifests itself when people blame the system for difficulties that may well be caused by other factors. Some people may just want to have 'nothing to do with the system'.

These reactions against a new computer system may stem from a number of reasons, largely historical, but they will have to be corrected or allowed for if future computer applications are going to succeed. Users may regard the computer department as having too great powers, and controlling (by technology) other departments which were previously controlled by people within the user department. Computer people seem to have great status in the eyes of top management and are not governed by the same codes as the rest of the company. Pay scales seem to be much higher for computer staff, particular when seen in the light of the length of time that computer staff have worked with the firm. In any case, the track record of computer applications — missed cutover dates, greater costs, fewer benefits, and designs which seem to be very different from that promised - should have led to reduced salaries and status, not the opposite.

Some of these arguments are valid, others less 'objective', but the poor communications between computer staff and others in the organisation, caused by the use of jargon and a lack of training and education, have not helped. Somehow these barriers have to be broken down if computer applications are really going to succeed.

One way to help this process is to involve all members affected by computer systems in the computing process. This includes the top management of the organisation as well as departmental staff. In the past, top management has avoided much contact with computer systems. Managers have probably sanctioned the purchase of computer hardware and software but have not involved themselves with their use. They preferred to keep themselves at a 'safe' distance from computers. This cannot lead to successful implementation of computer systems: managers need to participate in the change and this will motivate their subordinates.

Attitudes are changing partly because managers understand this effect and partly because they can see that computer systems will directly help them in their decision-making. Earlier computing concerned itself with the operations of the firm, modern systems concern themselves with decision-support as well. Without decision-support systems, firms will lose out to their competitors. Managers are therefore far more likely to demand sophisticated computer applications and play a leading role in their development and implementation.

Communications between computer and non-computer people within the organisation must also improve. This should establish a more mutually trusting and cooperative atmosphere. Training and education of all staff in the organisation about computers are therefore important for the success of the computing venture. Of course data processing staff should also be aware of the various operating areas of the business. This should bring down barriers caused by a lack of knowledge and technical jargon and encourage users to become involved in the technological change.

Involvement should mean much more than agreeing to be interviewed by the analyst and working extra overtime hours as the operational date for the new system nears. If the users participated more, perhaps being responsible for the design, then they are far more likely to be satisfied with and be committed to the system once it is implemented. It is 'their baby' as well as that of the computer people. This environment is one where the users and analysts work as a team rather than as expert and non-expert. There is less likely to be a misunderstanding by the analyst which causes a poorly designed system. The user will also know how the new system operates by the time it becomes operational, with the result that there are likely to be fewer 'teething troubles' with the new system.

The role of the computer analysts may be more of *facilitator* than designer, advising on the possibilities from which the user chooses. This movement can be aided by the use of application packages which the users can try out and therefore choose what is best for them. Another possibility is for the user or the analyst (or both) to develop a 'prototype'. There are packages available which will set up screen layouts and bring in blocks of code for validating and presenting data. The users can compare all these possibilities and develop a prototype before making up their minds on a final design. This can then represent the specification for the new system. Prototyping is discussed fully in the next section.

A very interesting case study relating to a successful application of participation at Rolls Royce is given in Mumford and Henshall (1979). The approach recognises that the clerks who will eventually use the system ought to have a major design role. This includes the form of work structure into which the computer aspects of the system are embedded. The final system design is evaluated on the basis of job satisfaction of those working on it as well as its efficiency. A likely result of taking job enrichment into account is the reduction of monotony usually associated with the clerical tasks of computer systems. It is particularly interesting, however, to discover that a small group of white collar workers at Rolls Royce did not want an intellectually taxing job and provisions were made for them in the final design.

Mumford distinguishes between three levels of participation. Consultative participation leaves the main design tasks to the systems analysts, but tries to ensure that all staff in the user department are consulted about the change. The systems analysts are encouraged to provide opportunity for increasing job satisfaction when redesigning the system. It may be possible to organise the users into groups to discuss aspects of the new system and make suggestions to the analysts. Most advocates of the conventional approach to systems development would accept that there is a need for at least this level of participation.

Representative participation requires a higher level of involvement of user department staff. Here, the 'design group' consists of user representatives and systems analysts. No longer is it expected that technologists dictate the design of the system to the users. They have equal say in the decision. Representative participation does assume that the 'representatives' can represent the interests of all the users affected by the design decisions.

Finally, consensus participation attempts to involve all user department staff throughout the design and development of the system. It may be more difficult to make quick decisions, but it has the additional merit of making the design decisions those of the staff as a whole. This is the approach particularly favoured by Mumford. Sometimes the sets of tasks in a system can be distinguished and those people involved in each task set make their own design decisions.

One idea which supports a high degree of user participation is that of the **information centre**, which was proposed by IBM. By giving users ready access to appropriate tools and guidance from the data processing department, user departments could, it is proposed, develop systems themselves. A user request for a system *may* lead to standard data processing work — procedural language solutions, high volumes of data to be processed, critical response times ... and a long development time. But the user request may be followed by advice on how users can themselves make use of facilities available such as microcomputers, terminal access, query languages, and other packages such as report generators, graphics, spreadsheet, and file management systems.

One of the very positive aspects of the information centre idea is that it provides choice rather than immediate solutions (which may not match the requirements). A number of alternatives are provided and the user exercises choice between these alternatives which will have social as well as technical repercussions. User groups can discuss social issues such as retraining, new departmental structures and new job responsibilities as well technical issues such as terminals and the particular package required. In view of this, it should be a prerequisite for users to decide on the socio-technical objectives before approaching the information centre. Only then will the users be able to rank particular solutions.

There has to be a great deal of support from the information centre. It has to be a centre of education — what computers can and cannot do, the importance of good standards, security provision, and so on — as well as a source of training, reference material, and advice on particular problems and the appropriateness of particular hardware and software solutions. Data processing professionals are much more facilitators in this environment, though they may be brought in to assist on tasks such as detailed debugging.

In the first chapter we discussed the problems of the application backlog, where user departments may have to wait years for the implementation of systems. The information centre solution can speed up the development of applications and maintenance (as the users will maintain the systems as well as develop them). On the other hand, care has to be taken to prevent the scope of applications being limited, as users cannot be expected to know all the possibilities that computers offer. Furthermore, there is a danger that because of poor testing, documentation, validation, backup and recovery procedures, the quality of the final systems are poor. This will reduce the possibilities of sharing data, with consequent data duplication and the possibility of inconsistency. The role of the facilitators is therefore crucial. It should not be the intention of the data processing department to 'wash their hands of the systems' if the major role in their development rests with the users.

The participative approaches to information systems development discussed in this section are pragmatic but they require concensus on the part of the technologist and users. Sometimes the technologists may 'agree' to the approach but resent it: they feel that they have lost their power in the firm. Sometimes users resent the time taken from their usual work: they may ask why they should spend their time on 'computers' when they are employed to work on their application. But it is surely generally accepted that some level of participation is necessary whatever approach to systems design and development is adopted. Otherwise there is a very real risk that new systems will be rejected by the people who are expected to use it.

6.4   PROTOTYPING

We have seen that many systems are implemented but then rejected by the user department. One way to reduce this possibility is to develop a prototype first so that the users can see what the output of the final system could be like. If comments are unfavourable, ideas from the users can be implemented on the prototype until the users are happy with it. Sometimes users are unsure about what they want from the system, and the prototype solutions can guide them towards a knowledge of their requirements.

Frequently it is only possible to develop a prototype having some of the features of the final system. In any case, the analyst may only wish to examine areas where he is unsure of the user requirements or where he is unsure about how to build the system. To some extent, therefore, prototyping can be seen as an improvement in the techniques of systems investigation.

A prototype is frequently built using special tools such as **screen painters** which facilitate the quick design of VDU screens and **report generators** which can be used to design reports from files. These reports, which can be soft copy (screen) as well as hard copy (paper) reports, are expected to conform to the basic layouts offered by the system. This leads to an acceptable design in quick time. If the screen layout is not entirely satisfactory, the prototype can be quickly redrawn using the tools available. As with word processing systems, the gains accrue when making changes. Only the points to be changed need to be redrawn, not the whole screen.

Report generators may follow a question-and-answer session with the user which finalises on the basic data to be displayed on the report and also on the calculations required, such as averaging, summation, highest and lowest fields, and so on. Report generators will also set up page headings and page numbers for each new page. More sophisticated systems may have already prepared screens, such as a standard invoice or order form layout. They may have a sort and merge facility which will be used for report generation from a number of files. Report generators are usually associated with small files, but their elements are included in most commercial DBMS.

'Natural' is a development language which can be used alongside the Adabas DBMS to produce prototypes quickly where the data is held in the data base. IBMs VS APL is frequently used as a prototyping tool used alongside the IMS DBMS, although it does require some programming skill to use. Another tool called 'Maestro' is supplied by Philips and is described as a *programmers workbench*. This can be used to quickly build up programs from library-held programming constructs and so develop a prototype. Many of these facilities which can be used for prototyping are normally called *fourth generation tools* and we will look more closely at these in the next section of this chapter (and section 7.6).

Sometimes a microcomputer will be used to develop the prototype although the actual system will be run on a mainframe computer. Some packages are designed for microcomputer use. dBaseII can be used in this way to set up reports and enquiry runs from files.

Frequently a prototype system can be developed in a few hours, and it rarely takes more than 10% of the time to develop the operational system. This is surely a good investment of time if it means ensuring that the final version does provide the users with a system that they want. Some systems teams use the prototype as the user sign off. Once the users are content with the prototype output it will be the basis on which the actual outputs will be designed. This is likely to be a much better basis for a user decision than the documentation of conventional system analysis.

A possible drawback of prototyping is the likelihood that users question the time taken to develop the operational system when they know that the prototype was developed so quickly. This discrepancy will be due to a number of reasons. The final system will have to deal with all possible types of data and processing. The prototype may only have included the main types of data. The final version must be documented thoroughly. It needs to be programmed efficiently, whereas efficient coding of a prototype is not a prime concern. The validation routines in the implemented system have to be thorough. The users may need convincing that these considerations, which delay the system in their eyes, are necessary.

Some users and technologists could also argue that the time, effort and money spent in developing a prototype is 'wasted'. This is sometimes also said of user participation. It is sometimes difficult to persuade busy people that this effort does lead to an improved service from the computer department and it possibly needs management encouragement to provide 'weight' behind this argument.

Prototyping could be used as a basis for a methodology of systems development in the organisation. This may have an analysis phase which could use structured techniques to understand the present system and suggest the functional requirements of an alternative system. This can be used to construct a prototype for evaluation by users. In response to the resulting user comment, the prototype can be retuned and the process continue until the protopye represents the wishes of the user. Once this has been established, the target system can be designed and developed with the prototype being part of the systems specification.

Prototyping, used as an integral part of the systems development process, is discussed in Dearnley and Mayhew (1983).

Many prototypes are discarded as they will be inefficient and poorly designed and documented. They will not integrate into the other operational systems. The prototype may incorporate techniques which are impractical for the operational system. They are used only as a development tool. But as we have seen, a prototype may not always be developed as merely a learning vehicle. It could be used as part of the final system. The final prototype could be the basis for the operational system. The system has evolved by an iterative process. If this *is* the expected role of prototyping the analysts must be aware of robustness, documentation and efficiency when developing the prototype. The prototype must be able to handle the quantities and variety of live data that is unlikely to be incorporated in the test runs which are used to give the user an idea of the systems output and capabilities. Otherwise there is danger that prototyping will not improve the quality of systems analysis.

Used carefully, however, prototyping can help systems development in a number of ways. It is possible to test ideas without incurring huge costs, allow the user to look at a number of alternatives and see the opportunities that information systems can provide. Further by reducing the application development time and costs, it may make the acceptance of the final system more likely.

6.5   FOURTH GENERATION TOOLS

The term fourth generation systems can be applied to packages which are designed to help end user computing *and* to those packages which make systems development easier and quicker. This definition therefore includes prototyping tools. Conventional programming languages, even 'high level languages' like Cobol, Fortran and Pascal, have to be written by trained computer people and programs take a long time to design, code and test. Fourth generation languages are often referred to as 'very high level languages' because they should be easy to use.

We have already mentioned a number of tools that are often associated with the fourth generation — prototyping tools, query languages, report generators, program generators, documentation tools and data dictionaries.

Some of these systems are designed for end-user computing. They may feature a dialogue which approaches a natural language dialogue or a menu so that user requirements can be established easily. From the users' point of view, menu-driven systems are likely to be more easy to use than command-driven systems where the user has to remember a number of commands or refer to a 'facts-card'. In Fig. 6.5, the users process a number of menus to indicate which system and which part of the system they require to use. The options are provided in the menu: the user has only to select the option required by pressing the appropriate key (following the ?).

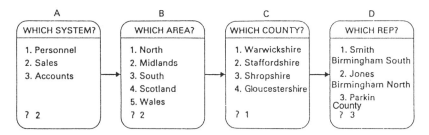

Fig. 6.5. Sequential menus.

Alternative approaches which are also easy to use include a soft copy form presented to the users who 'fill in the forms' to state their requirements (see Fig. 6.6) or icon/mouse systems, which use graphical symbols representing such requirements as filing (file cabinet), deleting (wastepaper basket) and so on. The user specifies the option required by pointing the mouse to the symbol and pressing a button to activate that process.

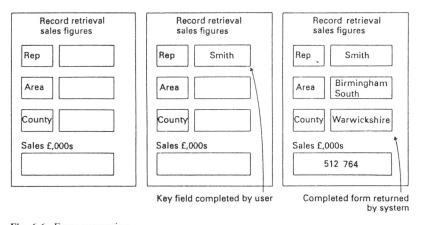

Fig. 6.6. Form processing.

Another set of tools, in this case more often appropriate to the computer professional (but not always), are the programmers work-bench and systems workbench. A **programmers workbench** usually provides a number of stock programming constructs (subprograms) which can be assembled to make a finished program. Some of these components will set up screen displays which can be 'tuned' by the individual user. The system will adapt the program coding according to the users' changes. The use of such packages speeds up many of the mundane elements of programming and could well be used as a protoyping tool.

An **analysts workbench** frequently includes the automation of some aspects of the structured systems analysis and design methodology discussed in section 6.2. These facilities include the automatic production of data flow diagrams with links to the underlying data base and automatic documentation. Maestro, mentioned in the previous section, can be used to generate programming code from Structured English. These facilities may also help the production of a prototype as well as the final version of the system. Some systems set up a **system encyclopedia** which stores information about the system being developed, information about the hardware used as well as application needs. It is mainly used as a documentation tool.

Together these 'fourth generation facilities' may be referred to as an **Integrated Programming Support Environment** (IPSE). The BIS/IPSE, for example, is a set of tools, techniques and documentation aids including:

(a) a formal approach to systems development,

(b) automated tools relating to documentation production and verification, and

(c) automated tools relating to project environment,

designed to help managers and users, and the systems analysts, designers and programming team. To help documentation management, for example, frameworks are provided for each type of documentation so that they ensure standards are adhered to. The 'flesh' in documentation has to be provided by the appropriate person at each stage through the life of the project, cross referenced and verified so that all aspects have been completed. These verification tools include checking that all sources and destinations in a data flow diagram have been defined, all functions can be supported by the entities and relationships defined in data analysis, entities defined are in third normal form, and so on. Further, automatic diagramming tools are provided and there is a library of standard symbols. The IPSE aims to provide a standard for project development and provide tools to ensure projects are developed faster.

We return to fourth generation tools in chapter 7 where an emphasis is given to aspects relating to data base management, and chapter 9 which is exclusively devoted to data dictionary systems. As well as being a store of information about the data base, a data dictionary system can be used to store information about programs and applications. Further, it can also store source code to be used when developing programs, generate test data for testing programs before they are implemented, have a query language and report generator interface, and hold validation routines for data to be added to the data base.

REFERENCES

Crowe, T. and Avison, D.E. (1980) *Management Information from Data Bases.* Macmillan, London.
> Chapter 10 looks at problems of user dissatisfaction and ways of increasing the likelihood of success by participative means.
Dearnley, P.A. and Mayhew, P.J. (1983) 'In Favour of System Prototypes and their Integration into the Systems Development Cycle', *Computer Journal,* **26** (1) (1983).
> Argues for prototyping being included as standard in the conventional approach.
DeMarco, T. (1979) *Structured Analysis and Systems Specification.* Prentice Hall, Englewood Cliffs, N.J.
Gane, C. and Sarson, T. (1979) *Structured Systems Analysis.* Prentice Hall, Englewood Cliffs, N.J.
> These two books cover the subject of structured analysis and its associated techniques.
Martin, J. (1983/84) *Fourth Generation Languages,* Vol. 1 (1983) and Vol. 2 (1984). Savant Research Institute, Carnforth, Lancs.
Mumford, E. and Henshall, D. (1979) *A Participative Approach to Computer Systems Design.* Associated Business Press, London.
Wood-Harper, T.W., Antill, Lyn and Avison, D.E. (1985) *Information Systems Definition: The Multiview Approach.* Blackwell Scientific, Oxford.
> This methodology emphasises participation and prototyping in information system development.

Chapter 7

Data Base Management Systems

7.1 INTRODUCTION

This chapter examines data base management systems (DBMS). These are software packages which manage large and complex file structures. DBMS make data bases available to a large number of users and the sharing of data can reduce the average cost of data access as well as avoiding duplicate and therefore possibly inconsistent or irreconcilable data. Data bases hold large amounts of data and operations required on them are complex. Correspondingly, DBMS are large, complex pieces of software. Users of data bases do not directly access the data base. Instead they access the DBMS which interprets the data requirements into accesses to the data base, makes the accesses required, and returns the results to the user in the form that the user requires.

In Fig. 7.1 the logical schema represents the view of the overall data base seen by the data base administrator. Codasyl called this overall view the *schema*. The different ways in which the various users view the data base, or at least 'their' part of the data base is correspondingly called the *sub-schemas*. In some systems (for example IDMS, section 7.3) the data definition language to set up the schema is different from that to set up the sub-schemas.

The various users accessing the data base via the DBMS may be user department managers and clerks as well as data processing professionals

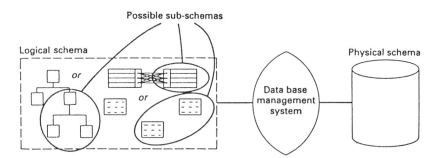

Fig. 7.1. The logical system and the data base management system.

146

and they may well use different sub-schemas. They may access the data base using 'user friendly' query languages on their VDUs. Access may also be made via user programs written in a conventional programming language such as Cobol or PL/1 which act as *host languages*. The subset of the host language which is used to access the data base is usually called the *data manipulation language*. IMS and IDMS have this host language access.

These host languages are procedural and the programmer has to know the set of logical procedures required to fulfil a particular request. This requires an in-depth knowledge of the language, but if the knowledge of the language has been acquired, the requests for data base access need not be complicated. Query languages are usually non-procedural and are usually suitable for untrained computer users and for 'ad hoc' enquiries of the data base. The most well known query languages are perhaps SEQUEL and QBE which were mentioned in section 4.2 and will be discussed further in section 7.2. A useful distinction between programming languages and query languages is to look at the former as concerned with the '*how*' of an operation, and the latter as being concerned with the '*what*'. One area of possible confusion is that 'query' languages are badly named in that they do usually offer ways of updating (changing) the data as well as accessing it in the form of a query.

There are a number of formats for the interface between the query language and the user. Many use special commands which are easily learnt. Others require the user to choose between options in a series of menus. These clearly make available the choices open to the untrained user, although they are consequently less flexible than some alternative ways of specifying user requirements. Some DBMS require the users to state their requirements on a soft copy 'form'. In some systems this form may be filled in using a light pen on the screen rather than by using the more conventional keyboard.

Perhaps the most 'user friendly' are those which use a near natural language interface. However there are lots of 'false friends', as natural language is ambiguous, and computers require unambiguous input. Such systems presently require long and tedious clarification dialogues. Although query languages can be easy to use and are usually geared towards fast response, they can be less flexible, perhaps rather limited, and usually less efficient than conventional programming languages.

Many of the better DBMS provide a number of ways of access. This is surely a good thing as there are many types of user. Users can be untrained and intermittant in their use of the system. These 'casual users' should not be required to be familiar with the system and usually do not want to be trained in its use. They should be encouraged by its ease of use. Skilled users may make frequent perhaps daily use of the data base and are usually willing to learn a simple syntax, though they are mainly concerned with the information that computers can give them, rather than the computers themselves. Other users will be computer professionals who will apply their long experience as computer and data base users, and be concerned about efficiency.

Many DBMS provide report generators as an alternative way of using the data base. Report generators are usually designed for unskilled users. They are oriented towards providing large volume printed reports rather than displays on the screen although many systems will happily 'print' the same report on the screen. The report format should be easy to design. Sometimes the DBMS will also provide program and system generation facilities. These can be used to build more complex systems, containing significant processing facilities. These features are normally associated with fourth generation systems (section 7.7). Query languages and report generators are unlikely to provide this power.

An important human intermediary will be the data base administrator (DBA) who will be responsible for the design of the overall data structure (schema) and for ensuring that the required levels of privacy, security and integrity of the data base are maintained. The DBA could be said to be the manager of the data base and, because the design of the data base involves trade-offs, he will have to balance these conflicting requirements and make decisions on behalf of the whole organisation, rather than on behalf of any particular user or departmental objective.

The data model which we have called the conceptual schema was developed independently of both machine and software considerations. This means that an 'ideal' data model can be formulated with the knowledge that it can be mapped on to a DBMS. Its conversion to a logical schema can then be made and this will be in the form required by the particular DBMS used, usually a set of relations, hierarchies or networks. Some DBMS accept more than one data model type, for example both relations and hierarchies. The DBMS will also take care of physical mapping onto storage media and file organisation. This may be carried out using instructions from the DBA, who will choose between the alternative file organisation methods offered by the DBMS as appropriate for the particular data.

These aspects are not the concern of the applications users. The DBA is involved in these decisions so as to ensure that the system is efficient. The separation of the physical storage structures from the user gives the user a high degree of **data independence**. This means that the user is screened from decisions regarding storage structures and access strategies (the physical structure). It also means that if a data item type (say a field called customer name) is added to the data base it will not be necessary to change programs that use the data base, apart from those that are directly interested in the customer name. With conventional systems, all programs accessing a file containing a changed data structure (the customer file in this case) will have to be modified and recompiled.

This data independence means that even when the pointers, character representation, record blocking, or access method are changed, this is not noticed by the users. Data independence is normally seen as one of the great advantages of DBMS. The degree of data independence will depend on the particular DBMS but will at least imply that the user will be screened from changes in physical location of the data, changes in parts of the schema which are not of interest to the user, and changes in the form of the data held. The appropriateness and sophistication of the data dictionary will also effect the degree of data independence of the system.

There are other advantages of the data base approach which offset their cost and the complexity of setting them up. The degree of data duplication may well be reduced significantly. The DBA should be aware of any data redundancy and be able to control it and ensure that any inconsistencies between the data are eliminated. There may be data duplication for good reason. If the same data is frequently required in two formats, it may well be efficient to store the data in both formats. Another example of efficient data duplication occurs where aggregations are stored. This aggregation may be accessed frequently and therefore it is more efficient to store the aggregation than to calculate the total from its constituent elements each time it is required. The important point is that the redundancy is known to the DBA.

A DBMS may facilitate access to the data by a number of users who may be using different host languages and query languages. The sharing of data reduces the average cost because the whole community pays for the data. New applications ought to be able to use the data base conveniently. They may require separate sub-schemas to be set up, but the data base will probably cater for the data needs of the new applications. As we shall see in later chapters, the role of both the DBA and the data dictionary are very important in fulfilling this function.

The data base approach makes it possible to exercise a high degree of control in the use of the data resource. This control will help to maintain the quality and integrity of the data and allow security measures to be enforced. The DBMS is likely to provide help to the DBA in the form of validation checks, logs, and copying facilities which will enable a successful restart should the system fail. Reports will also be provided which help the DBA maintain an efficient data base.

In the following sections we look at a number of DBMS either because they are used in a number of installations or they are particularly interesting. A thorough discussion of the facilities of any DBMS would take a book in itself and therefore only a 'flavour' of the systems can be given here. Further, it is not intended to be a 'best buy' survey. Some features that are mentioned in regard to one DBMS are available in others but are not mentioned again to avoid repetition. Emphasis is placed on three aspects: the logical schema (relational, hierarchical or network); physical schema (the file organisation(s) supported) and the query or host languages available to the user. This overall picture is shown in Fig. 7.2.

There are of course many criteria that ought to be used in evaluating DBMS, and the user interface, logical model type and file organisation supported are emphasised here because of the nature of the text. Other important criteria are mentioned below:

Cost: The cost of the software package itself but also the cost of extra CPU (central processor) power, extra main memory and backing storage which are usually necessary to ensure the efficient running of the data base.

Adaptation Required: Although generalised DBMS are intended for most users, there will be some work required in adapting it to the particular installation and installing it. This will have cost and time implications. In this text we have ignored 'tailor made' DBMS, that is, user-written data base systems. Situations are rare where this would be more efficient than the purchase of a generalised DBMS package.

Help to Data Base Administrator: DBMS are usually large programs and can be slow and memory-hungry. Most systems provide usage statistics so that performance can be monitored. Some provide facilities so that alternatives can be simulated. This will enable the DBA to see which is the most efficient. A further consideration is the help that the DBMS gives the DBA to enforce standards of data base use. Its relationship with the data dictionary system is also important. Some DBMS

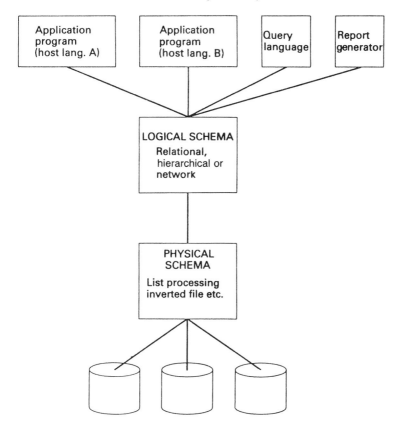

Fig. 7.2. Assessing a data base management system.

have a data dictionary interface and the DBMS/DDS/DBA are expected to work together. Connected with this is the level of support that it offers to ensure that access cannot be gained by users who have not got access rights. This will help to maintain the integrity (accuracy) of the data and the privacy of confidential information. The DBMS must also have good security features so that recovery can be made from a malfunction of the hardware or software.

Flexibility: Some DBMS are very flexible in that they can be used in batch or real-time mode, can be used by a number of types of user, and can run on a number of operating systems and hardware configurations. Data base use will vary over time as the company expands or applications change. It is important that the investment in one DBMS is not lost because of such change.

7.2 IMS

IMS is representative of a hierarchical system. It is one of the most widely used DBMS available. IMS is a large package which has data base management, communications management, and other features. Like most texts, however, IMS will be equated with the data base system. IMS has been marketed by IBM since 1967 and the company has improved the system over the years so that a data dictionary, data base design aid, performance analyser and monitor are now available.

The users' access to the data base is made via IMS commands in DL/1 which will be embedded in a host language such as Cobol, PL/1 or IBM assembly language. IMS does not have an integrated query language: access to the data base is made using a user-written program. However IMS can be used with the packages APL and GIS which will provide the required query language interface. An alternative hierarchical DBMS called System2000 does have an integrated query language and the user need only know the System2000 commands to access the data base.

The DL/1 programs will include the users' particular view of their part of the data base (sub-schema). This will be translated by IMS into the schema, referred to in IMS as the 'physical data base'. The use of the word physical in this context is perhaps misleading as there is a further mapping to the files on disk. This does mean that there is a significant degree of data independence — the user does not see how the data is held on disk storage.

As for the physical storage of data, IMS provides for a number of file organisation methods: sequential, indexed sequential, indexed direct access, and direct access. The large number of options add to the complexity of the system, though they are usually specified by the DBA and therefore this need not be looked on as a fault. System2000, mentioned earlier, is a hierarchical system that uses only one method, that of inverted files. These are also offered by Adabas, which is discussed in section 7.5.

In IMS terminology, each hierarchical structure defined to it is called a data base. Each record type in the structure is called a segment type. Thus for each IMS data base, there will be a root segment type followed by a number of child segments. In the original 'pure' hierarchical version of IMS, no child segment type could have more than one parent segment type — m:n relationships could not be specified. The occurrences of the root segment must be ordered, but the occurrences of child segments need not be ordered. Figure 7.3 illustrates the IMS data model and its associated terminology.

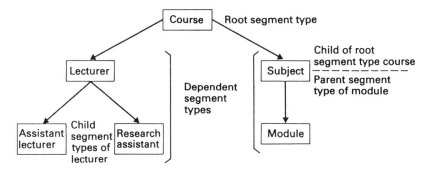

Fig. 7.3. A physical data base type: course details.

In the figure, COURSE is the root segment type. LECTURER is both a child of the root segment type and parent of the ASSISTANT LECTURER and RESEARCH ASSISTANT segment types. These are child segment types of LECTURER. SUBJECT is a child of the root segment and parent of MODULE. Figure 7.4 shows one occurrence of the physical data base which relates to the MSC1 course. Another occurrence is implied by the MSC2 root segment.

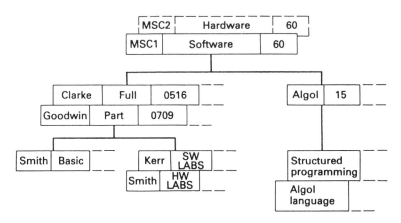

Fig. 7.4. Sample physical data base occurrence (another occurrence is implied by MSC2 root segment).

In later versions of IMS the strictly hierarchical approach has been contravened to allow users to link IMS data bases. If, for example, there are two data bases set up, one for courses and another for lecturers, the user might want to connect these as shown in Fig. 7.5. The link between the LECTURER segment type and the SUBJECT record type gives the latter two parents. In IMS terminology, COURSE, being on the same data base, is said to be the 'physical parent', and LECTURER the 'logical parent' of SUBJECT. SUBJECT is the 'logical child' of LEC-TURER and the physical child of COURSE. The structure is still limited as a segment type can have only one logical parent as well as only one physical parent. But this solution to the situation where two trees share a common segment type avoids some data redundancy.

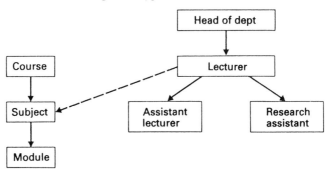

Fig. 7.5. IMS — logical parent.

Each of these physical data bases is defined by a Data Base Description (DBD). This is usually set up by the data base administrator. In the DBD the data base and then each segment type is named. The size of the segment followed by details of all the fields (data elements) belonging to the segment are then provided. The sequence of these statements is important as that of the segments in the DBD reflect the hierarchical structure.

```
1   DBD      NAME=COURSEDB,ACCESS=HIDAM
2   SEGM     NAME=COURSE,PARENT=0,BYTES=31
3   FIELD    NAME=(COURSENO,SEQ,U),BYTES=4,START=1,TYPE=C
4   FIELD    NAME=CRSENAME,BYTES=20,START=5,TYPE=C
5   FIELD    NAME=CRSELGTH,BYTES=3,START=25,TYPE=C
6   SEGM     NAME=LECTURER,BYTES=31,PARENT=COURSE,BYTES=57
7   FIELD    NAME=(LECNAME,SEQ),BYTES=25,START=1,TYPE=C
8   FIELD    NAME=LECTIME,BYTES=4,START=26,TYPE=C
9   FIELD    NAME=LECTNO,BYTES=4,START=30,TYPE=C
10  SEGM     NAME=ASSTLECT,BYTES=25
-
20  LCHILD   NAME=(SUBJECT,SUBJNO)
-
34  DBDGEN
35  FINISH
36  END
```

Statement 1 in the DBD names the data base as COURSEDB and gives its access method (in this case HIDAM, or hierarchical indexed direct access method). Statement 2 names the root segment (COURSE) and gives its length in bytes. The root segment is the only segment that does not have a parent (parent=0). Statements 3 to 5 define the fields of a segment — their name, length, starting place in the data base definition and type (characters in this case). COURSENO has been defined as the field for ordering the data within the root segment. Thus record occurrences within the COURSEDB will be ordered (SEQ) in ascending value of COURSENO, which will be unique for each segment occurrence (U means unique). The alternative (M) means multiple, which implies that there can be more than one occurrence of the given segment type under a common parent occurrence.

The number of bytes specified gives the size in characters of each segment and field. This method of specifying the field sizes is somewhat machine-oriented. Child segments may be in a particular sequence if required (the LECTURER segment is ordered). The DBD and DBDGEN statements mark the beginning and end of the physical data base description. FINISH and END are instructions to the IMS control programs to end the IMS job. IMS sub-schemas are defined in a similar (though not in exactly the same) way.

The hierarchy is specified by the sequence of the statements, from top to bottom and left to right. In Fig. 7.6 the sequence follows the pattern of starting at the root segment and goes next to 2, being below it and to the left. As 2 is not at the bottom of that path, control passes below and to the left of it to 3. This is at the bottom of the path, so control passes to the parent of 3 and below right to 4. This segment is at the bottom of that path and its parent 2 is then called. This has no more paths to the bottom right and control passes to the root segment 1 and thereby to 5, 6, 7, to 8, back to 7 for 9 and back to 7 and then 6 for 10. At this point all the segment types have been processed.

Once the hierarchy has been set up it is possible for users to access, update, add and delete the data using the DL/1 language within the host language program. The DL/1 statements in the data manipulation language (this term is not used by IBM) are extensions to the host language to call the data base. The GET statement in the Cobol extension is used to access data on the data base and can be in one of many forms, partly due to the complexities of hierarchies themselves. The GET UNIQUE (GU) retrieves the segment directly, at least it appears that it does to the user but it may be retrieved actually via a search through pointers. GET NEXT (GN) retrieves the next record in the hierarchy according to the

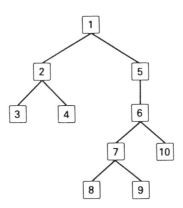

Fig. 7.6. IMS — hierarchical sequence.

hierarchical sequencing scheme discussed above. GET NEXT WITHIN PARENT (GNWP) follows sequential segment retrieval under the current parent occurrence. This type of command allows a user to navigate around a data base using the access paths that have been defined in the Data Definition Language. Unlike relational data base systems, all access paths which might be needed have to be specified in advance of the data base being constructed.

If it is required to REPLACE (REPL) or to DELETE (DLET) the segment, it must first be HELD to prevent others accessing it before the alteration is made. The GET statement becomes a GET HOLD statement such as GHU, GHN or GHWP. The add command INSERT (ISRT) is also used for data base maintenance.

IMS offers a number of alternate ways to map the data structures to storage devices. These include sequential, indexed sequential, direct access and indexed direct access. A particular access method has to be chosen for each physical data base (hierarchical data structure). Hierarchical Sequential Access Method (HSAM) provides sequential access to the entire data base and is intended for magnetic tape files and is not therefore widely used. For the indexed sequential method (HISAM) the root segment type key is the prime key and it is also possible to allow the child segments of the root segment to be indexed or accessed sequentially.

For the direct access method (HDAM), the user has to supply a convenient randomising algorithm to be applied to the key of the root segment. In the case of a HIDAM file (indexed direct access), the root segments are stored in ascending order of key and accessed in a separate index. Other, lower level segments, are stored and accessed using pointer chains from their parent segment. Backward pointers are also catered for if required by the users.

Thus, although HDAM gives better direct root access and update time, root segments cannot be accessed sequentially by key as in the case of HIDAM. The range of choice does give the data base administrator a considerable workload. Fortunately IMS provides tools which can help the designer by simulating the performance of IMS under different load conditions and design parameters. This design task is critical for the efficient working of the system.

Postscript — DB/2, SEQUEL and QBE

IMS has been available for many years and because of the investment that IBM and many IBM users have in the system, it is likely to be around for some time to come. However, IBM have also made available the relational data base system called SEQUEL (or SQL) which is a non-procedural relational language (see section 4.2). This can be used in application programs or interactively (ISQL). This is not too dissimilar to QUEL, discussed in the context of Ingres in section 7.5.

A further facility, Query by Example (QBE) is also available and is provided along with SEQUEL in the data base system DB/2 which has recently been made available. IBM has apparently spent considerable effort in providing 'migration' facilities so that IMS data bases can be transferred to DB/2.

QBE is particularly interesting in its user interface. A run could begin with the user requesting a particular relation (say EMPLOYEE) and be presented with the bare relation structure:

EMPL NO	NAME	STATUS	PAY/DATE	TAX/DATE	SALARY

The user can request details of the tuple with employee number 756 by completing that entry. The user also marks with P (for print) any other entries for that employee that are required:

EMPL NO	NAME	STATUS	PAY/DATE	TAX/DATE	SALARY
P:756	P	P			P

The system then returns:

EMPL NO	NAME	STATUS	PAY/DATE	TAX/DATE	SALARY
756	SMITH	FULL			12000

Joins of relations are effected by including in the user request fields from more than one relation.

7.3   IDMS

IDMS is probably the leading DBMS to be modelled on the Codasyl Data Base Task Group (DBTG) proposals and is available on IBM, Univac and ICL computers. It is capable of handling network data structures as well as hierarchies. IDMS terminology is similar to that used in the Codasyl reports. The record or record occurrence is the basic unit of addressable data which is itself sub-divided into data items. Similar record occurrences belong to a record type and related record types belong to a set type where one record is the owner and others are members. The records in a set are linked together using pointers. The owner points (NEXT) to the first member and so on. A chain is established because the last record points to the owner record. There may also be backward pointers (PRIOR) and pointers for all member records to the OWNER.

Hierarchies are established by a member (a record type) of one set being the owner of another set, indeed it can be the owner of a number of sets. Networks are established because multiple membership is allowed as well as multiple ownership. IMS's extension allows only one secondary membership. IDMS supports m:n relationships using the link records discussed in section 4.4.

The schema is set up using the schema DDL commands, and this provides a complete description of the data base. It names and describes all the areas, set occurrences, record occurrences, data items and data aggregates (groups of data items) that exist in the data base. An example of part of a DDL run follows:

SCHEMA NAME IS WHOLESALER.
AREA NAME IS SUPPLIER-AREA.
PRIVACY LOCK FOR PROTECTED UPDATE.
AREA NAME IS CUSTOMER-AREA.
PRIVACY LOCK FOR EXCLUSIVE RETRIEVAL.

```
RECORD NAME IS SUPPLIER
        LOCATION MODE IS DIRECT SUPP-NO
                DUPLICATES ARE NOT ALLOWED
        WITHIN SUPPLIER-AREA.
        02      SUPP-NO            TYPE IS CHARACTER 8.
        02      SUPP-NAME          TYPE IS CHARACTER 25.
        02      SUPP-ADDRESS       TYPE IS CHARACTER 75.
        02      SUPP-AMNT-OWING TYPE IS INTEGER 10.

RECORD NAME IS CUSTOMER......etc.
```

You will note that the AREA concept has been retained by IDMS although it was dropped by Codasyl in its 1978 Report. The record occurrences are stored on a page, which is a convenient, user-specified, unit of storage. These pages are grouped together into the area, a sub-division of the overall data base. The privacy clause can be associated with each area so that they may be protected for retrieval or update or both. The clause is also available at the record level.

A record's allocation to a particular page is located by one of the following 'location modes': CALC, VIA, and DIRECT. If the CALC option is used, the record occurrence is stored on a page calculated by IDMS using a hashing (randomising) algorithm. The VIA location mode places the record on or near the page containing its member record. This location mode is particularly suitable where the retrievals of the record type are carried out primarily as a member of the named set. If the DIRECT location mode is used, as in the above example, then the record is placed on or as close as possible to a user (that is, application program) specified page in an area. These location modes were specified in the original Codasyl proposals but dropped in the 1978 Report because, like the area concept, these are physical aspects of the data base and do not relate to its logical design.

Some records on the data base may be required directly for some applications (CALC) and sequentially (VIA) for others. The DBA may exercise the power of assigning priorities to the conflicting procedures and choose the option with the highest priority. Another possibility is to use the option VIA and create an indexed set with the key of the record

as the owner, and the actual record as the member. This will improve retrieval times, but it does cause added complexity in the updating procedures. This trade-off between retrieval times and updating speed ought to be a prime consideration when defining set relationships.

Having set up the areas and records, it is necessary to describe the relationships between the records by set definitions.

```
SET NAME IS PURCHORD-SUPPLIER
        OWNER IS SUPPLIER
        ORDER IS SORTED BY DEFINED KEYS
                DUPLICATES ARE NOT ALLOWED
        MEMBER IS PURCHASE-ORDER
                INSERTION IS AUTOMATIC
                RETENTION IS FIXED
        KEY IS ASCENDING PONUM IN PURCHASE-ORDER

SET NAME IS PURCHORD-PRODUCT
        OWNER IS PURCHASE-ORDER
        MEMBER IS PRODUCT.......etc.
```

This definition is followed by END SCHEMA.

The first line names the set and the owner and member records of the set are named. Duplicate values for keys are not permitted in this particular set definition. The order statement specifies where member records are 'placed'. This is a logical not a physical placement. The INSERTION statement defines rules for record creation and the RETENTION statement defines rules for record retention. The key is used as a sort control for a member record of a sorted set.

Set membership can be explicitly established by a CONNECT statement. If set membership is automatic, the member record is made a member of the set whenever an occurrence of a member record is stored in the data base using the STORE statement of the DML. Another aspect of set descriptions is the way in which records are placed in a set. They can be ordered and the order FIRST indicates that new members are placed at the beginning of the list. Member records can also contain pointers backwards (PRIOR) and to owner records. There is also a privacy mechanism for a set and there can be a lock for FIND, ORDER, INSERT or REMOVE.

Each record in IDMS is actually divided into two parts: a prefix area, which contains the pointers necessary to maintain the data relationships with other records, and the data area. Each record is connected by pointers to the other records in a set occurrence. The pointer consists of the page number and the line number of the stored record. In fact the Device and Media Control Language (DMCL) was not specified in the Codasyl proposals and is defined in IDMS in order to set up the mapping of the logical pages described above to physical blocks on disk and other physical considerations. Its exact format will depend on the particular hardware used.

As well as the SCHEMA DDL, IDMS (like Codasyl) provides a SUBSCHEMA DDL for Cobol which consists of a:

TITLE DIVISION, which names the subschema and identifies the underlying schema;

MAPPING DIVISION, which defines the aliases which the user wishes to give to sets, records, and data items;

STRUCTURE DIVISION, which has three sections as follows:

REALM SECTION, the realm being the logical subset of the schema data base,

SET SECTION, which lists the set types, and

RECORD SECTION, which list all the schema records required by the user, with details of the items in the records, such as type and length.

The list is followed by the statement END SUBSCHEMA.

IDMS, then is similar to the Codasyl proposals in most respects having a schema and subschema data definition language which are processed by three 'compilers'. The term compiler here is not inappropriate as the language specified by Codasyl does not seem totally unfamiliar to applications programmers used to Cobol Data Division formats. However, much of the terminology, for example, sets, areas, and schema, will be new to Cobol programmers not working in a data base environment because the original Cobol language is file-oriented, not data base oriented.

Although the Codasyl DBTG proposed a host language data manipulation language embedded originally in Cobol, IDMS has added to this basic system a report generating system called IDMS/CULPRIT which will write reports on the contents of the IDMS data base and an ON-LINE QUERY FACILITY. Nevertheless, IDMS is essentially a host language system. Access to the data base by applications will normally be made using Cobol, PL/1 and other languages having a

'CALL' statement. The programs are preprocessed by an IDMS preprocessor before compilation in the host language. This changes DML commands into IDMS subroutine calls.

The IDMS DML commands correspond very much to the Codasyl data manipulation language proposals with one or two minor changes such as the addition of a command OBTAIN (which is a combination of FIND and GET in Codasyl terminology). FIND and GET can still be used separately. The FIND function locates the required record occurrence and GET puts it into a user-defined working storage area.

Unlike IMS, which does not have OPEN and CLOSE statements because they are carried out automatically by the IMS system, IDMS has four control statements: INVOKE, OPEN, CLOSE, and IF. The sub-schema is specified by the INVOKE statement and the OPEN statement makes available areas within the sub-schema to be accessed. The OPEN statement has a number of options depending on the type of access (update, retrieval), and the levels of protection which will depend on whether other users should be locked out whilst the present user has access. The CLOSE statement closes all areas previously opened and the IF statement tests if a set occurrence is, or is not, empty.

The FIND statement (or, if preferred, the OBTAIN statement) has a number of options depending on the type of access. The direct access form is:

FIND record name RECORD USING keyname

Within a particular set or area, the FIND statement can include NEXT, PRIOR, LAST, nth (an integer), or FIRST record of a particular set or area, or OWNER of a set. The options NEXT or PRIOR relate to the record presently being processed: the next record on the list or the previous record. The options FIRST, LAST or nth refer to that particular record in a set or area. The OWNER locates the owner record in a set.

Each pointer requires four bytes and therefore one record occurrence participating as a member of two set types requires pointers to owner, next and prior for the first set type and next and prior pointers for the second set type, a total of 20 bytes reserved for set linkage. GET FIRST and GET LAST can be processed by going through a number of GET PRIOR or GET NEXT statements.

There are also five modification statements in the IDMS data manipulation language (DML). These are STORE and DELETe (for adding or deleting a record on the data base), MODIFY (to replace a record in the data base), INSERT or REMOVE (to make or cancel a record as a member of an occurrence of a set type).

The facility of locating a particular record is, like IMS, complex because of the way a record is searched for in the set structure. However, IDMS has the particular advantage of being based on the Codasyl proposals which is a well-respected standard for DBMS. In addition, it provides a number of routines for the data base administrator, on-line access and the report generator Culprit.

7.4   ADABAS

Adabas has been used by such major British corporations as ICI and British Rail. It is not possible to classify it according to relational, hierarchical or network although it can be used to support all three logical data structures. It does use tables although there is no 'official' relational data manipulation language. Tables are joined (or 'coupled' in Adabas terminology) on a common attribute. This also allows hierarchies and networks to be defined to the data base.

Like many other DBMS, it has opted for a host language DML, again those languages having a CALL facility. However, there is a query language provided called 'Adascript'. The data is mainly stored physically as partially inverted files, although direct access may be used to retrieve records. It is an unusual system in that when records are added to the data base they are allocated a permanent internal sequence number (ISN) which is used both to access records and to couple files. Adabas also compresses data so that the extra storage overhead for ISNs is not evident. Thus spaces in an alphabetic item or leading zeros in a numeric item will be compressed out of data held in storage but edited in again for users when accessed by them.

In Fig. 7.7, the inverted list shows the internal sequence numbers of the keys. There is one occurrence of Jones (ISN is 3) and three occurrences of Brown (ISNs of 1, 4, and 6). The inverted file may provide the answer to a query (for example 'How many people called Brown are on the data base?'). If the record is required, the ISN is converted to an actual address via the address convertor (ISNs 1 and 2 are in block 1) and so the data records can be accessed.

When a file is set up, it is possible to define repeating groups of variable size so that each record may have zero, one or many occurrences of the group. In a Cobol group item, as for many programming languages, the group has to be of a fixed size. Even more unusually, for both a record and a field within a group, it is possible to define a 'multiple value field' such as a part description which may consist of a

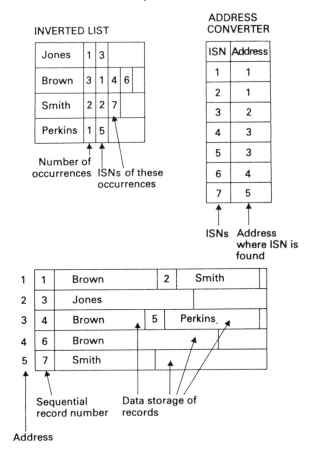

Fig. 7.7. ADABAS record storage system.

number of words. This enables the user to retrieve the full description even though only part of that description was known.

To set up data relationships between records it is necessary to define one or more keys (called 'descriptors') which ensure its inclusion in the index. A descriptor can be a field, a number of fields or a part of a field. A record type may have one or more descriptors. Files can be coupled on the basis of this descriptor. Two files are listed below. If Student Number is a descriptor of both, the coupled search 'What are the names of students who passed the exams?' could be made. Table (file) 2 can be used to find the student numbers of those who passed, and with these descriptors, their names can be obtained from Table 1.

Table 1

STUDENT NO	NAME	ADDRESS

Table 2

STUDENT NO	PASS/FAIL	

If name on Table 1 and pass/fail on Table 2 were also made descriptors, that is kept in the inverted files, the above request could be fulfilled without access to the data storage areas.

If files are coupled so that a particular value of a descriptor occurs once on one file and a number of times on another, a hierarchy is defined. If another value of the same descriptor occurs more than once on the first file and once on the second, a network is described. Adabas does not differentiate — and checks are not made — to ensure that particular key values are not repeated.

Data manipulation via a host language is achieved using a CALL statement with parameters which will specify: the command to be executed, file number, format of records or fields to be retrieved, space for the record retrieved, information on the search itself (the boolean operators AND, OR, BUT NOT, TO (value) of top field value required), and the descriptor values. The command can specify any sorting that is to be carried out before returning the values. The number of ISNs satisfying the enquiry is returned and this enables the user then to choose whether only some or all of the 'hits' need be retrieved. Records may also be accessed in physical storage sequence (as opposed to the particular FIND command described above) or in descriptor sequence.

The privacy and security features of Adabas are thorough. For example files and fields can be protected against unwarranted access by passwords and these may be 'scrambled', that is ciphered so that a copy of the contents of the storage area would not help in searching for a password. Users are given an authorisation level for a file and a field. There is a separate allocation for access (read) and update (write). These can be any level between 0 (lowest) and 14 (highest). Similarly each field and file has a security level. For access rights, the user's access level must be greater than or equal to the security level. As protection is given to the field as well as file, a user may be able to access a logical file (e.g employee), but not a particular element within it (e.g salary).

7.5 INGRES

Ingres (Interactive Graphics and Retrieval System) is a relational data base management system which is designed to run on the Unix operating system. Unix can run on minicomputers and larger microcomputers, usually known as 'supermicros'. The data manipulation language on Ingres is Quel (QUEry Language). This language is based on the relational calculus described in section 4.2. Ingres also has report writer and query by forms facilities.

Memory is allocated by the CREATEDB command and files are organised in a hierarchical fashion with a root file and a number of other files in that subdirectory. Once this data base has been set up it is possible to access the data base through the Unix command 'Ingres *dbname*'. A file, that is a relation, could be set up by:

CREATE PRODUCT(PRODUCT-NO=I4,PROD-DESC=C25,...)

where I is for integer and C for character attribute. Integers are for numeric data not having decimal points and characters are non-numeric data such as names and addresses. A third possibility is F for floating point, for numeric data with a decimal point. If the cost of the product was included in the PRODUCT relation, then this would be defined floating point. The integer can be 1, 2 or 4, depending on the number of bytes the item requires. A one byte field can hold numbers between -128 and $+127$; 2 bytes between -32768 and $+32767$; and 4 bytes between -2147483648 and $+2147483647$.

Data can be added to each file (relation) by displaying the relation on the screen:

PRINT PRODUCT

\g

which will give:

PRODUCT RELATION

PROD-NO	PROD-DESCRIPTION

and then appending the list of values of each occurrence:

APPEND TO PRODUCT(PROD-NO=476000,
                          PROD-DESC="CAMERA"....)

which will give:

PRODUCT RELATION

PROD-NO	PROD-DESCRIPTION
476000	CAMERA

Alternatively, it is possible for Ingres to input data from an external file using the COPY command. This is less laborious to use and much more suited to large file updates. The data file is created separately and, once checked, can be copied into the Ingres file:

COPY relationname(domainname=format,...)FROM datafile

COPY PRODUCT(PROD-NO=I,PROD-DESCRIPTION=C)
FROM FILENAME

A way of inputting data which is easier for the user is by using a facility which designs VDU 'forms'. The form is set up according to the layout of the relation and one tuple can be entered at a time.

The Quel commands are set up in a user workspace until the user passes the requests to Ingres with '\g'. The RANGE command preceding instructions reduces the amount of typing by abbreviating the relation names, for example,

RANGE OF P IS PRODUCT

When Ingres receives the \g, it executes the Quel command or commands. It is frequently useful to store a series of commands as a file to be executed when appropriate. This avoids setting up the same set of commands on each run. One Quel command has already been used, the PRINT command which can be used to list a number of relations on the screen. By attaching a printer to the terminal, this can be used to echo what is 'printed' on the terminal to print on paper. Perhaps the most important Quel command is the Retrieve command which enables data to be retrieved from the data base in the form of a relation. It permits a full range of arithmetic and boolean operators. An example of the retrieve statement could be:

RETRIEVE (P.PROD-DESCRIPTION) WHERE
P.PROD-NO=1565678

PROD-DESCRIPTION
WIGITS-300

Details about relations can also be obtained using:

HELP
\g

which will list the relation names and the 'owner' (creator) and if the

HELP is used along with the particular relation name, such as:

HELP PRODUCT (or HELP P)
\g

the system will give the user of the relation the following information:

RELATION	PRODUCT
OWNER	AVISON
TUPLE WIDTH	144
SAVED UNTIL	MON SEPT 15 1985
NUMBER OF TUPLES	477
STORAGE STRUCTURE	PAGED HEAP
RELATION TYPE	USER RELATION

ATTRIBUTE NAME	TYPE	LENGTH	KEYNO
PROD-NO	I	4	
PROD-DESC	C	25	

This could be very useful to the data base administrator who could also use the RESTRICT ACCESS command to prevent unauthorised access to sensitive data. As with most systems, there is password control. The integrity of the data base can be helped by giving a range of valid values when entering data:

INTEGRITY P.PROD-NO < 00030000

The command end \g stands for go and there are other abbreviations for commands such as \p for print (the contents of the memory buffer), \i for include followed by the filename, \e for edit the buffer, \r for reset (which clears the buffer) and, finally, \q for quit the Ingres run.

We have described the Quel query language. Ingres also has Query by Forms (QBF) and a report writer. QBF allows simple functions to be performed on an Ingres relation, but retrievals requiring multiple relations are not supported in QBF. It is menu driven and this allows the user to add data to the data base (Append), change the data (Update) and view the data (Retrieve). A form is put on the screen by:

QBF database name relation name

for example,

QBF ORDER PRODUCT

TABLE IS PRODUCT
product no:
product description:
quantity in stock:

and

      RETRIEVE 764

would fill in the details of the product number 764. A part-completed description could be used using the 'wild card' facility. QBF could look for a match on

      NAME="AVIS*".

The report writer facility gives a formatted listing from a data base. It is particularly useful for summary reports.

7.6   FOURTH GENERATION PACKAGES

Fourth generation systems normally include a DBMS as one of a number of tools which support development work. These systems include Nomad2, RamisII, Mimer and Oracle. A discussion of their data dictionary features is given in section 9.5.

Nomad2

This consists of a relational DBMS with report writer, graphics, statistics, procedural language and financial analysis package in a single environment. It aims to give high productivity of applications development and prototyping. The package runs on IBM mainframe hardware, but there are related packages which can run on microcomputers for end-user application development and which can be connected to a mainframe for file transfer. The data base itself is described by a schema (and the relations can be shown graphically or by a list) and it has security and integrity features. Although designed on relational lines, the system facilitates the setting up of hierarchies as well.

The report writer can be used for setting up standard formal reports and is mainly intended for end users. The graphics part can display data in terms of bar charts, scatter diagrams, and pie charts. The statistics package can be used for regression analysis, t-test, and chi-squared tests as well for working out minimums, maximums and averages of data in the data base. Nomad provides a procedural language which can be used as an alternative to conventional programming languages.

RamisII

This is similar to Nomad2 in that it has a relational-like DBMS and also supports hierarchies. It runs on IBM hardware and interfaces with conventional programming languages as well as having its own non-procedural language. A report writer and statistics, spreadsheet and graphics programs are part of the overall package and it can be linked to an IBM PC for end-user use and for data transfer to and from the main data base.

Prototypes are set up in Ramis using the non-procedural language. The user specifies what data or action is required, not how it is achieved, and what form the results should take. The end user may request a report. A report lay-out is 'suggested' by the system and, through a process of refinement, the prototype frames are established. Totals, subtotals, headings and row and column placement all have default values for the easy creation of standard forms but can be changed where necessary.

Mimer

This system also has a very high level language provided and is therefore much easier to learn than, say, Cobol. Again it uses a relational data base. It can run on a number of computers. The tools provided include a program generator, query language (which is similar to IBMs SE-QUEL), screen handler (to set up data entry and menu screens quickly), and information retrieval facility (for large data and text search) as well as conventional programming language access. It includes security, backup and privacy features and allows multi-user access.

Prototypes can be developed using the program generator and, when the user is satisfied with the prototype, convert this version into fast machine code for efficient operational running or into Cobol or Fortran if this is preferred (as these will be more portable). These programs are generated by the system on request and can be run on other machines with an equivalent compiler. Statistical, graphics and other packages are integrated into this fourth generation 'toolkit'.

A package, which like Mimer is available from Savant and can interface with Mimer, is Data Designer. The DBA is expected to design the data base in terms of third normal form relations and the system can generate from this model a number of reports and graphical output, including the data structures themselves. A similar package, Everyman, is discussed in section 8.3.

Oracle

This system is also based on a relational DBMS with SQL as the query language interface. Other tools include a host language interface, applications generator, report writer, and word processor. The applications generator works by a question-and-answer dialogue which allows screens to be set up for data entry and validation, query and update applications. The report writer is used to generate reports from the underlying data base. Again, to ease its use there are a range of default options which can be changed where appropriate. A 'rough' prototype display can therefore be produced very quickly and altered as necessary. The word processing facility allows the integration of text and graphics output.

REFERENCES

There are a number of texts on data bases and these look at the systems in much more detail than has been possible in this chapter. These include:

Cardenas, A.F. (1985) *Data Base Management Systems*, 2nd edn. Allyn and Bacon, Boston.
Date, C.J. (1981) *An Introducion to Database Systems*, 3rd edn. Addison-Wesley, London.
McFadden, F.R. and Hoffer, J.A. (!985) *Data Base Management.* Benjamin/Cummings, Menlo Park, California.
Vasta, J.A. (1985) *Understanding Data Base Management Systems.* Wadsworth, Belmont, California.

Lobell, R.F. (1984) *Application Program Generators — A State of the Art Survey.* NCC, Manchester.
Martin, J. (1983, 1984) *Fourth Generation Languages*, Vols. 1 and 2. Savant Research Institute, Carnforth, Lancs.

Chapter 8

Microcomputers, Distributed Data Bases and Data Base Machines

8.1 INTRODUCTION

There are a large number of file management systems available on microcomputers. A file management package, along with a spreadsheet and a word processor, is often bought with a new microcomputer. Frequently these three packages are provided 'free' with the micro-computer. There are a number of file management packages, including DMS Delta and dBaseII, which work with the CP/M operating system and 64k of main storage. Such systems allow the user to set up files and update records and support information retrieval. Usually, results are displayed on a VDU, but most will also produce reports on hard copy. Frequently the user wishes to select particular records from a file and sort them. A typical request could be to select from a customer file those customers who live in the North East region, to sort them in ascending order of credit balance, and to display the results on the monitor.

Although many file management systems allow the user to set up files containing a thousand or more records, they may be limited, for example by restricting the user to process only one file in any run. This proves convenient for straightforward applications but is very restrictive in the context of applications discussed in this text. Readers should be aware that some 'data base' systems on microcomputers are of this type. Furthermore, many do not provide any separation of the logical and physical models. In other words, what the user sees is what is held on disk. There is no data independence, there is only one version of the file and the users are not cushioned from changes in data storage. Even the best systems should only be regarded as file management systems with some data base management aspects.

Nevertheless there has been a steady improvement in facilities. For example, whilst dBaseII allows a maximum record size of only 1000 characters, dBaseIII allows 512,000, and whilst dBaseII only allows two files to be open at one time, dBaseIII allows ten files to be open. However, dBaseIII needs the power of a 16 bit microcomputer, such as an ACT Apricot or IBM PC.

Since the advent of 16 bit microcomputers in 1983, which have been gradually replacing the 8 bit, 64k microcomputers, it has been possible to purchase rather more sophisticated data base packages. These microcomputers have a much greater internal memory capacity, and have much faster processors. The standard internal memory is 256k for most 16 bit microcomputers, although many can be expanded to three times this size. Disc storage technology on modern microcomputers is also more sophisticated. The floppy disks on these micros are designed to have four times the storage capacity of the previous 'generation' (microcomputer generations are separated by about four years). Some systems usea high density flexible disk having a capacity of half a megabyte (half a million characters) or more. Hard disks, having a capacity of 10 or 20 megabytes and upwards are also available with these computers. This book is stored on a 10 megabyte disk and backed up on a three and a half inch floppy disk. Along with the improved hardware, improved operating systems such as MS-DOS have made genuine data base management much more feasible.

During 1984, 'supermicros' became widely available and these can have an internal memory of a megabyte or more. Hard disks with a capacity of over 100 megabytes can be attached to them. These systems allow a number of users, frequently 8 or 16, to use the computer at the same time. The operating system, most frequently Unix, can run powerful DBMS as efficiently as many minicomputers. The Ingres application discussed in the appendix was implemented on such a computer. It is therefore not incongruous to discuss data base management in a microcomputer environment.

In this chapter we look at the development of microcomputer data base packages. We consider the facilities that could be expected in a basic and a more sophisticated file management package on microcomputers. Another option that is considered in this chapter is that of distributed data bases, where the data base is held in a number of locations and can be used, at least in theory, by anyone on the computer network. We also look at data base machines, computers dedicated to data base use.

8.2   FILE MANAGEMENT PACKAGES

There are many file management packages available on microcomputers. Some have been designed specifically for microcomputers: perhaps for a particular microcomputer such as the Apple Macintosh, Apricot or IBM PC, or for microcomputers running on a particular operating system such as MS-DOS.

Some packages are based on data base systems that have proved successful on minicomputers and mainframes. MicroRapport, for example, is a scaled down version of the relational DBMS Rapport. Users who are used to data base systems on larger machines are likely to notice a degradation in performance as well as limitations in their facilities. These could take the form of limitations in the maximum number of fields per record, the maximum number of records per file, the number of files that can be accessed simultaneously, or in their security provisions.

Whereas most mainframe data base systems are hierarchical or network because these systems developed in the 1960s and early 1970s when relational data bases were only in the realm of the researcher, most microcomputer file management and data base systems are relational. Only in the late 1970s, when coincidently microcomputers were being marketed in a big way, were relational data bases commercially available. Relational systems are also considered much easier to use and are therefore particularly suitable for microcomputers.

Micro Data Base System (MDBS) is an exception, being a network system which attempts to follow the Codasyl recommendations as near as possible on an 8 bit microcomputer. It also has backup and privacy features and interfaces with Cobol, Fortran and Pascal. Concepts such as 'sets', 'owners', and 'members', familiar to Codasyl users are all used in MDBS. Unlike the original Codasyl specification, which requires many-to-many relationships to be supported by the use of link records, MDBS will support these relationships directly.

Frequently, microcomputer data bases have query languages far more 'user friendly' than the equivalent mainframe system. Microcomputers have been sold to the general business user rather than to computer professionals, and so this is perhaps not surprising. Data can be input using a question-and-answer session with the user. Alternatively, data can be entered by means of setting up a table or filling a VDU 'form'. Rarely is the user required to have an in-depth knowledge of computers or any knowledge of a conventional programming language.

dBaseII

dBaseII is a well established file management system used on microcomputers running under the CP/M operating system and useful for the storage and manipulation of small files which are seen by the user as relations. dBaseII files are set up using the CREATE command — the system is command-driven. This is unusual as most microcomputer systems are menu-driven.

> CREATE
> ENTER FILENAME: Product
> ENTER FILE STRUCTURE AS FOLLOWS
> FIELD NAME,TYPE,WIDTH,DECIMAL
> OO1 Prod-no,C,8
> OO2 Prod-nme,C,24

The system prompts the user to type in the name of the file, and for each field, its name, type, width, and decimal. The type relates to whether the field is character, numeric or a logical. If it is numeric, the user types in the number of decimal places. The width is the number of characters in a field.

Once the file structure is established, dBaseII prompts the user to enter data for the file by providing its structure for each record in turn. The user completed the blanks.

> RECORD 00001
> PROD-NO| |
> PROD-NME| |

The file can then be processed by the USE statement. Data can be added (APPEND or INSERT), changed (EDIT), listed (LIST and DISPLAY), sorted (SORT), searched for (FIND and LOCATE), and data items can be manipulated arithmetically (COUNT, SUM, TOTAL). Relational, logical and string operators can be used to enhance the capability of the commands. The commands can all be abbreviated to four letters.

A user can interactively interrogate the data base or set up a command file. This is useful if a particular routine (set of commands) is executed daily or weekly. The command DO causes the commands in the specified file to be executed.

Once a data base is in 'use', the user may go to the top or bottom of the file by specifying GO TOP or GO BOTTOM respectively. To find a specific record, the user may use:

> LOCATE FOR name = Williams AND age = 21

and if the LOCATE is successful, this record can be DISPLAYed on the monitor. Where a file is INDEXed, then FIND is a more effective command than LOCATE as it will retrieve the record 'directly' (though an index) rather than processing through the file serially.

Each relation is stored as a dBaseII file. Although it is a relational system in that files are presented to users in a tabular form, only the JOIN, of the relational algebra statements, is supported. There are other limitations which will be seen by users who are used to mainframe data base systems. In particular, only two files can be open at any one time. The package cannot handle arrays of data which makes the handling of all but the most trivial sets of data difficult. The maximum number of characters per file is 255; the maximum number of fields is 32; and the maximum number of records is 1000. These points should not be read as criticisms of the package, more as an illustration of the limitations of systems of the last generation of microcomputers.

Everyman

Another interesting package for microcomputers is Everyman. It is interesting in the context of this text because it includes data modelling features as well as having an integral data base management facility. When setting up a data model, the user names the relations and the system draws boxes around these. The next step is to show the links between the relations, and so the data structure is set up. The simple model shown as Fig. 8.1 has three entity types and the hierarchy implies that a COURSE can *consist of* many MODULES and a LECTURER can *teach on* a number of MODULES. This structure, with entities, links and relationship names (called link names) is drawn by the user interactively usually using a mouse.

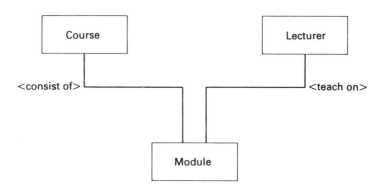

Fig. 8.1. Everyman — data modelling.

As the structure is being drawn, the user can also set up the relations (described as in the documentation as 'identical, fixed format card boxes') with attribute details. Fig. 8.2 shows such a structure: the MODULES that are found in a particular COURSE occurrence. You will note that details of the COURSE tuple are given along with the details of the modules in that course.

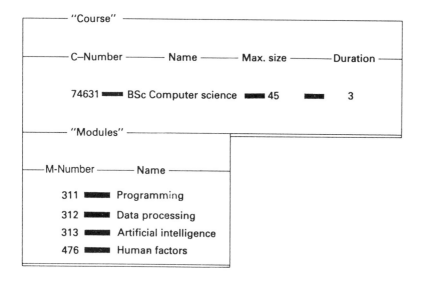

Fig. 8.2. Everyman — relation details.

It is possible to query the data base using various selection criteria such as 'those tuples in MODULE where 'm-number' is greater than 311'. An expression can be constructed consisting of a number of operators for selecting tuples (for example $=$, $<$, $>$ for equals, less than and greater than), and operating on the results (for example $+$, $-$, $/$, $>?$ for plus, minus, divide and maximum of). The expressions can be complex with logical ANDs and ORs and NOTs.

The system has comprehensive help facilities, as would be expected for a microcomputer data base package and could be used by users and data processing people as a data base design package, data base management package and as a prototyping tool. In the latter role, once the users were satisfied with the design, it could be used as the basis for the mainframe version. Alternatively if the limitations of the microcomputer hardware were not important (in terms of memory size, speed, and a limited multi-user facility) the prototype could 'become' the operational system.

8.3   DISTRIBUTED DATA BASES

Sometimes shared data can be distributed in a number of locations or machines in the same location. In one arrangement, each location stores the data which originates at that location, but the data can be accessed by users at other locations. This means that not only is the data base distributed, but so is the intelligence of the system. The users at different locations are not just terminal users. They have intelligent machines with software to perform general data processing as well as software to access the data base.

With personal computers on most office desks, it seems reasonable to link the 'data base' on each machine so as to avoid duplicating the collection, validation and storage of data. It also avoids the necessity of having to access the corporation mainframe, which may be undesirable because of time delays, expense, and the dependance on the data processing department. Users could be linked by a local area network (see Fig. 1.8) but the arrangement needs to be changed so that the users' data bases are accessed by all users on the network.

Ideally, the user is able to formulate a request to the distributed data base and receive a reply unaware of the location of the data required to answer that request. The data base is looked on as a single data base. This level of data transparency is difficult to achieve because it requires a global conceptual schema describing all the data on the distributed data base, and the supporting software will be costly and complex.

One possible configuration is shown as Fig. 8.3. Most application programs and packages will set up and use data provided by the local data base facility. However there is also a need to access the data bases of other departmental computers through the network. The user will need to have access rights to these other systems. In this configuration there is no notion of a central computer. In an alternative approach, a microcomputer with a data base and data dictionary facility could be part of the network for the use of all users and therefore be seen as a central data base. But there may also be the capacity for users to access external data bases when required.

The distributed data base may not be based on a microcomputer network. On a much larger scale, the IDMS distributed data base supports IDMS running on IBM mainframes on each of the distributed data base sites.

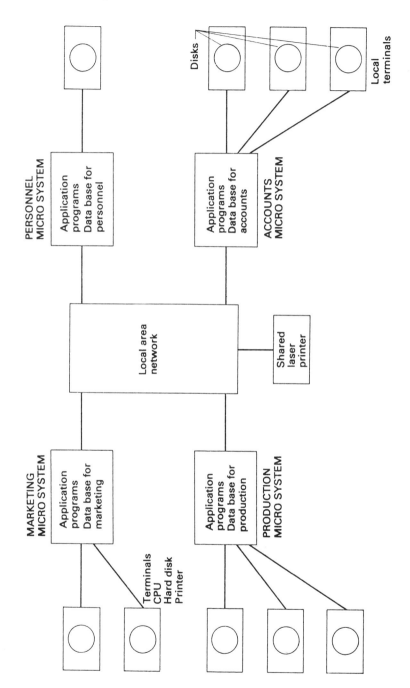

Fig. 8.3. Distributed data base.

Local Authorities Management Information System (LAMIS)

One successful arrangement for providing decision-support through distributed data base is the LAMIS design. It has been implemented by ICL on a number of local authorities including Dudley and Leeds. The data base used is IDMS on the ICL 2900 mainframe range of computers. Each application area of the local authority, such as Land and Property, Employees, and Population, has its own data base. Applications access this data base using application programs and query languages. LAMIS caters for conventional operations level processing of large amounts of data, on-line or batch processing of general enquiries, and complex management enquiries.

As can be seen from Fig. 8.4, the Land and Property application area has a number of systems to deal with rent invoicing and payments, rates

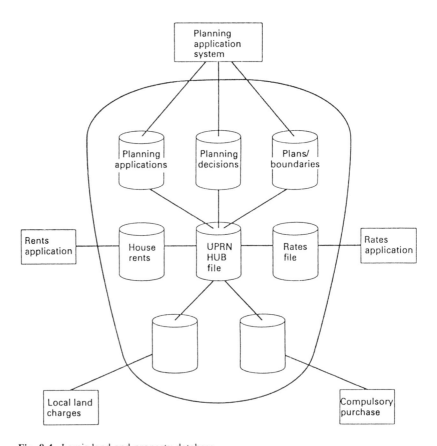

Fig. 8.4. Lamis-land and property database.

invoicing and payments, planning applications and compulsory purchase processing. Each of these applications has their own logical files. There is also a hub file which is referenced by all the files.

The *hub file* represents the cross-referencing for that application area. In the Land and Property data base, each index will uniquely identify a piece of land in the local authority area. This index is called a *Unique Property Reference Number* (UPRN). Houses, factories, planning applications, rents and rates can be cross-referenced using the UPRN system.

Applications relating to rents will have efficient access to the required part of the data base. Further, assuming that access rights are granted, the manager of the rents department has the opportunity to find out whether there are any planning applications associated with that house by using the UPRNs as an index to search the planning applications part of the data base. It also means that new applications can be added to the system and logical files linked in conveniently.

A UPRN is used rather than a house number and street number because these may change: a block of flats may be replaced by a house. The hub file will be able to convert UPRNs to an address and an Ordnance Survey grid reference, so that accesses using these as keys can be made into the system.

LAMIS is designed so that the local data bases need not be centralised but distributed. The hub files themselves can be cross-referenced. In this way, as shown in Fig. 8.5, users can have access to their own data base area, those of other application areas and even local authorities (if these are linked in the system).

8.4 DATA BASE MACHINES

A further possibility, not so far discussed, is that of data base machines such as the IBM System/38, ICL CAFS, Britton-Lee IDM and Amperif RDM-1100 (which uses the IDM). These are computer systems dedicated to data base use rather than general data processing. They are designed to make data base access as efficient as possible.

Conventional hardware is designed more for numerical calculation than for data base operation. One solution, shown in Fig. 8.6, is to keep a conventional computer for standard processing, but connect to it a data base machine. This could ensure that data sent to the host computer has been pre-processed to provide only the data required to answer a particular query. A conventional system would retrieve a large amount of data from backing storage and then process this data to filter out the

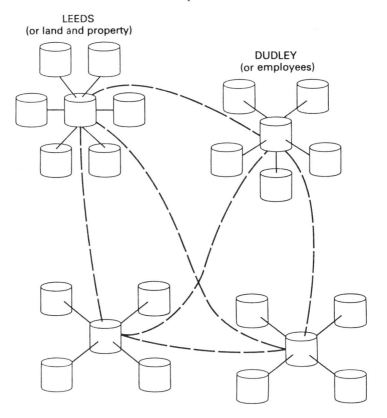

Fig. 8.5. Linking of hub files of different data base areas, data bases or local authorities.

relevant data in order to fulfil the information request. This consumes a significant amount of the computer's processing power which can be avoided.

Further, with data base machines, it is possible to perform many of the functions previously carried out by software on the dedicated hardware. Such computers can be connected to one or a number of general-purpose computers. Alternatively, a stand-alone computer can be used which will carry out conventional processing but has been designed to make data base processing particularly efficient. The IBM System/38 is a system, based on a powerful minicomputer. This system uses micro-coded data base instructions to improve on data base access times.

An alternative design for a data base machine uses content-addressing. Data base requests normally refer to data by its content (for example, where course='computing') not its address. Conventional

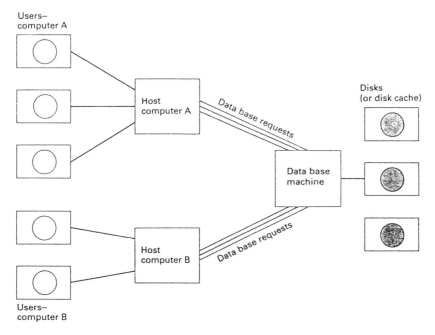

Fig. 8.6. A back end data base machine supporting multi-host systems.

computers have to convert this to an address. Content-addressable processors are designed to perform this task as efficiently as possible. The ICL CAFS system (CAFS = Content Addressable File Store) is such a product. Parallel content-addressable processors facilitate the operation of a number of data base transfers at the same time. The files form an integral part of the hardware of such a data base machine. In conventional systems the files will be held on a comparatively slow device such as a conventional disk drive.

Dedicated systems may also have more advanced memory technologies, capable of storing massive amounts of data. Such storage includes bubble memories which might be used for a 'disk cache'. This is slower than main memory, but considerably faster than conventional disk storage.

The Interactive Database Machine (IDM) of Britton-Lee is a back-end data base machine capable of processing a 1000 transactions per minute. Most of the data base operations are performed by a dedicated processor which increases the performance of the data base because of its specialised hardware and software. The IDM machine can be accessed by 64 types of host computer and uses a disk cache as described above. Online storage can be up to 10 gigabytes. It is modular in design having a data dictionary, concurrency control, security, backup and recovery features. The DBMS part is styled on the relational system SQL (see section 7.2). Being a data base machine it does not execute application programs which will be performed by the host machine, but the latter will be relieved data base processing.

REFERENCES

Avison, D.E. (1983) *Microcomputers and their Commercial Applications.* Blackwell Scientific, Oxford.
Discusses file management systems. The most up-to-date sources of information are the various business microcomputer magazines.
Cardenas, A.F. (1985) *Data Base Management Systems,* 2nd edn. Allyn and Bacon, Boston.
Chapter 16 contains an overview of distributed data bases and some useful references.
Hsiao, D. (ed.) (1983) *Advanced Database Machine Architecture.* Prentice Hall, Englewood Cliffs, N.J.

Chapter 9

Data Dictionary Systems

9.1 INTRODUCTION

There has recently been a significant increase in the use of data dictionary systems (DDS). This is mainly due to the corresponding growth in the use of data analysis techniques, DBMS and fourth generation products. Organisations frequently purchase a DDS along with a DBMS in order to record details of the data which will be held in the data base. Many DDS are integrated with a particular DBMS or offered as a possible 'extra' to a DBMS.

A DDS is a software tool for recording and processing data about the data (meta data) that an organisation uses and processes. Originally DDS were designed as documentation tools, ensuring standard terminology for data items (and sometimes programs) and providing a cross-reference capability. They have now evolved as an essential feature of the systems environment and are of particular importance to the data base administrator who will use the DDS to keep track of the data on the data base and to control its use. This helps to minimise maintenance and development costs.

Datamanager (MSP), ICL DDS (ICL), DD/D (IBM), UCC-10 (University Computing-10), Data Catalog2 (Synergetics), Data Dictionary (Applied Data Research), Control 200 (Intel), Predict (Software AG), Data Control System (Cincom), and Adabas DDS are some of the many DDS products available.

A DDS is a central catalogue of the definitions and usage of the data within an organisation. This can ease the sharing of data among applications. If used alongside a DBMS it could be said to be a directory of the data base, 'a data base of the data base', although this relationship might be better expressed as an 'information source about the data base'. Most DDS are used chiefly as a documentation aid and as a control point for referencing data. A DDS will hold definitions of all data items, which may be any objects of interest, and their characteristics. It will hold information on how this data is used as well as how it is stored.

A DDS may play an active role in systems design, programming, and in running systems. It could be used to provide the data structures to the program at compile time or validate data at execution time. It can be used as a storage base of programming code (subprograms) and these subprograms may be used in a number of programs. Many DDS are therefore more than mere points of reference and they hold information about processes as well as data.

However, the major benefit of most DDS stems from it being the central store of information about the data base. The DDS pervades all aspects of systems work and its use could lead to improved documentation and control, consistency in data use, easier data analysis, reduced data redundancy, simpler programming, the enforcement of standards and a better means of estimating the effect of change. Of course some of these advantages could be equally said to be the result of using a data base with a DBMS and an effective data base administration team. Indeed, they all contribute to an effective data processing environment. The influence of the DDS, as shown in Fig. 9.1 can pervade all areas of data processing: to users, managers, and auditors, as well as to data processing professionals and the data base administrator.

From the point of view of the organisation, management is now becoming more aware that the data of the enterprise is a valuable and important resource which must be properly managed. There must therefore be a knowledge of what data exists and how it is used. There must be control over modifications to the data base and the processes that use it. There must also be control over plans for new uses of data and over the acquisition of data. The DBMS may well achieve some of these objectives itself, but in order to gain full control over the data resource, it is necessary to collect and store information about the data.

The British Computer Society set up a working party (referred to hereafter as the BCSWP) to suggest a standard for data dictionary systems. Their report was published in 1977 and has proved the basis for the design of the DDS marketed by ICL. The BCSWP suggest that a DDS should provide two sets of facilities:

1. To record and analyse data requirements independently of how they are going to be met.

2. To record design decisions in terms of data base or file structures implemented and the programs which access them.

These two sets of facilities are referred to as the **conceptual data model** and the **implementation data structure** respectively, some writers referring to these as **management use mode** and **computer use mode**.

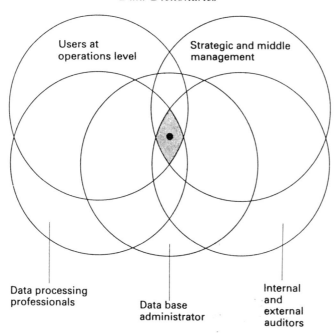

Fig. 9.1. Influence and users of data dictionary.

The conceptual view shows a model of the organisation, that is, the entities, their attributes, and the relationships between these entities. This model is the result of the data analysis process and is therefore independent of any data processing implications. The conceptual view can also include details of the events and operations that occur in the organisation. It represents therefore the conceptual schema — the end result of the data analysis exercise described in chapter 3.

The implementation view gives information about the data processing applications in computing terms. The processes are therefore described as systems, programs and subprograms (modules), and the data is described in terms of files, records, and fields, or in the terminology of the DBMS used (for example, segments, sets, and data items). Some systems also include an operations view as part of the implementation level. This will include information relating to the operation of the system, such as the schedule for running the system and its hardware requirements.

The BCSWP argue that one of the main functions of a DDS should be to show the relationship between the conceptual and implementation views. One view should map on to the other view. Any inconsistencies between the two should be detected. It should be noted, however, that many DDS currently available only support the implementation view and those which hold a conceptual as well as implementation view do not always map one to the other automatically nor carry out any checks to ensure their consistency.

The conceptual and implementation views for data and processes are shown in Fig. 9.2. The four quadrants represent the components of the DDS. There is a fifth component, mentioned before, which indicates the cross-referencing between components. Indexes can be used to identify entities, functions, and programs and this simple referencing system will be an effective tool in maintenance.

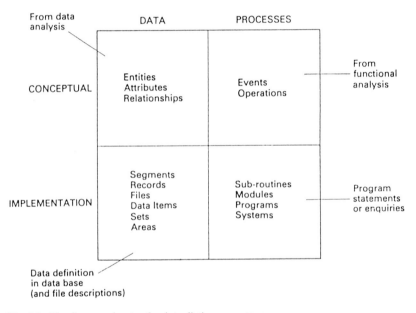

Fig. 9.2. The four quadrants of a data dictionary system.

For each data element, the DDS will contain amongst other things, the following:

★ The names associated with that element. There may be different names used by the various users and computer programs to refer to one element.

★ A description of the data element in natural language.

* Details of ownership (normally the department which creates the data).

* Details of the users that refer to the element.

* Details of the systems and programs which refer to or update the element.

* Details on any privacy constraints that should be associated with the item.

* Details about the data element in data processing systems, such as the length of the data item in characters, whether it is numeric, alphabetic or another data type, and what logical files include the data item.

* The security level attached to the element in order to restrict access to it.

* The total storage requirement.

* The validation rules for each element (for example the range of acceptable values).

* Details of the relationship of the data items to others.

With so much detail needed to be held on the data dictionary, it is essential that an indexing and cross-referencing facility is provided by the DDS.

Earlier DDS concentrated on documentation and on producing reports about the data on the data base. In installations where there are no DDS, computer systems can become entangled in a confusion of data. Data dictionaries are used to ensure greater discipline. Reports produced by the DDS are of use to the data administration staff who will attempt to improve the efficiency of use and storage of the data. These reports will also be useful to systems analysts, programmers and end users.

So that the user can request these facilities and to input data into the system, a pre-printed form usually in fixed format is provided by many DDS. There will also be some form of query language. Where a DDS is associated with a particular DBMS, then this will be the query language supported provided by the DBMS. The DBMS may assist in managing the data dictionary, indeed the data dictionary will be held on the data base, just like any other data base file.

Most commercially available DDS go beyond these basic facilities and the BCSWP sees the DDS as a tool with a number of objectives:

1. To provide facilities for documenting information collected during all stages of a computer project.

2. To provide details of applications usage and their data usage once a system has been implemented, so that analysis and redesign may be facilitated as the environment changes.

3. To make such access easier by providing cross-referencing and indexing facilities.

4. To make extension of the DDS easy.

5. To encourage systems analysts to follow structured methodologies.

This last objective could point, for example, to data dictionaries holding details of the contents of the sources and destinations (sinks) of data flows. In other words, data dictionaries are a tool of process definition as well as data definition.

The scope of a DDS is therefore broad. It is not merely a documenting aid: it is a support to all stages in the development and maintenance of a system and the control of the data base. A more sophisticated DDS will have a number of extra facilities such as the following:

1. Automatic input from source code of data definitions. These can be copied in at compilation time.

2. The generation of source code relating to items in the data dictionary to a sort program or applications program.

3. The recognition of several versions of the same programs or data structures may exist at the same time. The different versions could represent:

   * live and test states of the programs or data

   * programs and data structures which may be used at different sites

   * data set up under different software or validation routines

4. The provision of on-line facilities to aid the interrogation of the data base. Here, an interactive query language needs to be provided as part of the DDS.

5. The provision of an interface with a DBMS.

6. The provision of security features, such as password systems. These may be built in to restrict access to the DDS, for example, users should only gain access to that part of the data dictionary which is relevant to the job in hand. The ability to restrict the type of access, such as read, delete, write, and update, is as important to the DDS as it is to the data base.

7. The provision of facilities to generate application programs and produce reports and validation routines.

9.2 ADVANTAGES OF USING A DDS

A number of possible benefits may come from using a DDS. These include:

1. A DDS can improve the ability of management to control and know about the data resource of the enterprise. It can also show all the programs, files and reports that may be affected by any change to the definition or usage of data elements and possibly to generate code which reflects that change. It may be possible to assess accurately the cost and time scale to effect any change. A DDS also enables management to enforce data definition standards and also detect unauthorised use.

2. A DDS reduces the clerical load of data base administration. The form, meaning, and usage of data can be documented easier. It also gives the DBA more control over the design and use of the data base. Accurate data definitions can be provided directly to programs. Sensitive data can be made available only to particular users. Test and production versions of files and programs can be checked and the data base administrator can ensure that standards are being followed.

3. A DDS can aid the recording, processing, storage and destruction of data and associated documents flowing through an organisation.

4. A DDS can help systems development by generating test files and providing documentation.

5. A DDS provides application programs with data definitions and subroutines and therefore enforces some standards on programming, making programs more readable and consistent. This also removes much of the tedium associated with application program development.

6. A DDS aids application program maintenance because changes to the data and the data structures can be made where appropriate to all programs using the data. The DDS may itself document the change.

7. A DDS aids the operations side of computing by holding details of storage and recovery procedures, and archiving information. Some DDS provide job control parameters to run the systems.

8. A DDS may provide an estimate of costs of any proposed change of use of the data and estimate a time scale for making such changes.

9. A DDS can provide effective security features such as passwords to assist in the protection of the data resource.

In brief, the DDS will save development and operating time and reduce costs of the computing facilities. This chapter has looked at the possible features of a DDS, both the minimum features provided and those of a more sophisticated system. The following sections consider some prominent commercial DDS which are available and widely used.

9.3 MSP DATAMANAGER

Datamanager has been available since 1975. Whereas most DDS are expected to be run with a DBMS, Datamanager may be implemented without a DBMS, though it can interface with IMS, Adabas, and other DBMS. It is looked upon as a management tool for successful information management, rather than merely a data base for a data base. It is supplied as a 'nucleus' with a range of 'selectable units'. The choice of the selectable units will depend on the particular environment with which the DDS has to run. Facilities can be provided which enable it to run with Shadow or CICS which are systems supporting teleprocessing and a number of DBMS. A number of programming languages can access it. It also supports MarkIV, which is a file management and report generating system. There are other features such as security and user interface units which can all be added to the nucleus.

Datamanager fulfils four basic requirements:

1. To define corporate entities and their relationships.

2. To load these data, process and relationship definitions to the DDS.

3. To store and protect these definitions.

4. To provide an easy way of retrieving definitions in the manner required.

Datamanager can be used to hold information about files, records and items, whether they are stored on a data base or not. It also holds information about systems, programs and modules. All these are referred to as 'entities' and both data and process entities are held in a top-down manner with each higher level of data and process being able to refer to those below it. Thus an application system could be defined to the DDS as consisting of various programs each containing a number of subprograms (modules). It is also possible to specify relationships between these entities, cross-referenced with their DDS names.

By using a series of input commands, it is possible to create and extend the dictionary and there are also a series of housekeeping routines which maintain the dictionary. Datamanager can generate a number of types of report listing as well as deal with particular enquiries which may be as simple as:

'WHAT USES CUSTOMER-REFERENCE'

which would produce a list of all elements using an entity called 'CUS-TOMER-REFERENCE', to a more sophisticated

'WHAT USES CUSTOMER-REFERENCE
AND DELIVERY ADDRESS
BUT NOT DELIVERY DATE'

and

'WHICH PROGRAMS UPDATES EMPLOYER'

or

'WHICH PROGRAMS USES EMPLOYER'.

As well as having a full set of commands to query the DDS, the nucleus provides security against concurrent update and also error recovery facilities. It is also possible to add 'logical' dictionaries which provide each user with '*their*' version of the physical dictionary.

Datamanager does not provide a conceptual view of systems (one independent of the computer). This is true of many data dictionaries available including the Adabas and IBM data dictionary systems. Unlike Datamanager, these are both designed to work alongside a particular data base, Adabas and IMS respectively. Adabas DDS (ADADDS) is stored as a file in the Adabas DBMS. IBMs DDS is called the Data Dictionary/Directory (DD/D). It serves batch and on-line processing and works with IBMs assembler language, the IMS data base language DL/1, as well as the high level languages Cobol and PL/1. Like the other DDS discussed so far it supports the documentation of processes and data.

9.4 ICL 2900 DATA DICTIONARY SYSTEM

The ICL DDS is designed to take into account the conceptual as well as the implementation level. It therefore attempts to describe the business and the computer representation of data. It is modelled on the recommendations of the BCSWP. Further, the DDS is an important part of the ICL data analysis methodology. Many forms which are completed as part of data analysis are used as source documents for the ICL DDS. It is therefore used as a design aid as well as a documentation tool. The conceptual view which will be held on the data dictionary will include the entities, attributes, relationships, operations and events which define the data model. There is one form for each of these aspects of data modelling included in the ICL methodology.

At the implementation level, the view is represented by systems, programs and modules. It is in this respect rather similar to Datamanager. ICL DDS is expected to be run with IDMS which is the Codasyl-based DBMS discussed in section 7.3. The terminology and concepts for the data are associated with this type of DBMS. A schema is a description of the complete model; the sub-schema represents the various user views of the data base (subsets of the schema); a file is a collection of records; an area a collection of IDMS pages (the unit of filestore for transfer purposes); a record is a collection of logically related items (usually referred to as group items) and items, the basic unit of data.

Every element is described in the DDS by its properties including those which identify and describe the item, those which establish and describe links between items, administrative properties such as those which describe the various privacy levels required, and statistical properties such as the various access levels (peak and average frequency of access) to that particular item.

As well as having a command language, called Data Dictionary Command Language, to describe the data and processes, the system has powerful query facilities. The DDS allows interrogation through DISPLAY, ENQUIRY, LIST and PRINT. The DISPLAY statement can be used to give details of an element. Thus:

DISPLAY ENTITY STUDENT-TYPE ALL PROPERTIES

will give full details of a particular entity.

LIST EVENTS * DESCRIPTION

will list all events with their descriptions as contained in the DDS. The LIST command generates a list of all elements of a given type.

PRINT ALL ALL

prints the whole data dictionary.

ENQUIRY ENTITY STUDENT

will give details of entities, operations and attributes which use the entity 'student'. The ENQUIRY command is usually used to check on references between two specific elements or of a particular type or conforms to a particular search key.

The ICL DDS also has a free format command language which can be used to insert and edit items, and to update and interrogate, the data dictionary. The description of the data and information about its use are held on the DDS data base which is part of the IDMS data base. It therefore has the security and other features of IDMS.

Overall, the ICL 2900 DDS is a fairly sophisticated DDS and commands can be entered via a terminal and in batch mode. Its particular strong points are that it is part of the data analysis methodology as well as its closeness to the recommendations of the BCSWP. A number of packages have been developed by ICL to interface with the ICL DDS. They include Report Master and Query Master (for reports and user enquiries) designed for general users, there is a package Masterbuild (to develop the DDS) and Quickbuild (similar to Masterbuild, but containing streamlining facilities for quick set-up of small to medium systems).

9.5   FOURTH GENERATION/DDS

This section gives an overview of data dictionary systems included in some of the fourth generation systems discussed in section 7.7.

Oracle: Each time a relation is created, updated or deleted, the data dictionary is updated at the same time. The dictionary can be queried using SQL, the same query language as that used to interrogate the data base itself. It is in fact part of the Oracle data base, in the same way that the ICL DDS files are held in IDMS. Oracle DDS supports security privileges to prevent 'illegal' access, and only the user with data base administrator status can access details of these privileges.

Mimer: This maintains the definitions of the data items and relations of the Mimer data base. It also keeps information about users, such as their identity, authority level, and passwords (the latter being stored in a ciphered form). Again, the dictionary is held in the Mimer data base and, like Oracle, users can add their own specialised DDS tables relating to the data base which is not automatically provided by the system.

Nomad: The Nomad data dictionary N2DD is held on the data base and it is divided into a message file, help file, data definition and data sections. The first two sections contain the various warning/error messages and information to help the user. The data definition section describes the types of data items that are permitted in the data base, and the last section gives details of the data itself.

9.6 COST

Although the DDS is a very useful management tool there is a price to pay. The DDS 'project' may itself take two or three years. It needs careful planning, defining the exact requirements, designing its contents, testing, implementation and evaluation. This may take as long as the DBMS development project. This is not usually appreciated. The cost of a DDS includes not only the initial price of its installation and any hardware requirements, but also the cost of collecting the information, entering it into the DDS, keeping it up-to-date and enforcing standards.

Just as the use of a DBMS requires management commitment, so does a DDS. This is not always easy to achieve, particularly where the benefits are intangible and long term. Users have to accept that 'their' data can be shared and that they cannot be permitted to ignore the requirements of the organisation when wishing to reformat data, use different validation routines, or make any other move which might effect other users. Some users find conforming to the requirements of a DDS a 'nuisance' at best. This also implies commitment by management to the data base administrator function because the DBA is the focal point for setting good standards and enforcing them.

REFERENCES

British Computer Society (1977) 'Data Dictionary Systems Working Party Report', *ACM SIGMOD Record,* Vol. 9/4 (Dec 1977) or from BCS.
Curtice, R.M. and Dieckmann, E.M. (1981) 'A Survey of Data Dictionaries', *Datamation,* March 1981.
Gradwell, D.J.L. (1983) ICLs DDS, DD Update, BCS, April 1983.
Van Duyn, J. (1982) *Developing a Data Dictionary System.* Prentice-Hall, Englewood Cliffs, N.J.

Chapter 10

Data Base Administration

10.1 THE ROLE OF THE DATA BASE ADMINISTRATOR

Although this is the last chapter, it is one of the most important. The role of the Data Base Administrator (DBA) is crucial to the success of the data base and to the computer applications using it. The DBA should be involved in the planning of the organisation's data resource and in setting up the data base. Indeed the DBA ought to be involved in the evaluation of the basic hardware and software and be an important member of the systems planning team.

One of the main objectives of the data base approach is to facilitate the sharing of data between many users. But users may well resist both the DBA taking control of 'their' data and other users having access to it. This may lead to conflict. There needs to be a DBA with the necessary status to apply a corporation-wide perspective to mediate in such a conflict. Hopefully this will be achieved by facilitating communication between departments rather than by 'rule of law'.

There are a number of problems that may arise from the sharing of data. The balancing of conflicting interests requires a managerial perspective and a good knowledge of the business. Other problems require technical knowledge. The DBA will have to deal with complaints about usage of the data base and to provide technical training. These different aspects of the role of the DBA will be a constant theme in this section.

In practice, the DBA function needs to be carried out by a **team**. The director of this team needs to have sufficient standing in the organisation to remain independent of 'pressure groups' of data base users. The DBA is expected to be a good communicator and has to discuss aspects of data use and storage with managers, user staff, operations staff, and application developers. The DBA team also needs to have technically experienced people who have the responsibility for physical and logical data base definitions, implementing access rights, optimising performance levels, maintaining the integrity of the data base and general maintenance of the data base, the software supporting it and its use. The software will include the DBMS, the DDS and possibly some fourth generation tools as well. The team will also include people, whose role is to help train the users and help them with technical difficulties. Users will require this help no matter how 'user friendly' the system is supposed to be. Some members of the team will need to have a strong applications background to fulfil some user demands.

It could be said that part of the DBA's role is that of "public relations officer" for the data base. The problems relating to conventional systems need to be pointed out along with a description of the ways in which a data base environment might solve some of these problems. This education role may be followed by a training role. Should users wish to make use of these opportunities they will need more detailed help. The users may need assistance in understanding the data base structures and to derive a suitable subset which will provide for their data needs. Furthermore, this subset may need to be restructured for that particular application.

One of the main tasks of the DBA will be to load the initial data base, and this uses up considerable processor (and people) time. It also requires audit procedures which will be used to verify its success. Although much of the data will come from existing master files, there may be considerable re-structuring and re-naming. Some of the data will be newly held on computer.

The logical data structures will need to be changed over time according to the changing needs of the users. The DBA could be looked upon as a forward planner, as the data base can expand or be reorganised according to future needs and this has to be done with as little disruption to the present users as possible. It may be necessary to alter the way in which the data is physically stored on the data base. In this case the DBA will be involved so that the changes are carried out efficiently. This means efficient use of storage space and access time and reduced maintenance overheads. The DBA has to be aware of present and future needs and be aware of any advances in the hardware and software.

Efficiency of the data base is not a simple matter. There are a number of criteria which may conflict. Speed of access may conflict with efficient use of storage space. The DBA may aim towards 'satisficing' on a wide range of criteria, rather than optimise on any one criterion, in other words ensure that the performance of the data base on a wide range of issues is satisfactory.

Evaluating the performance of a data base is also difficult: is speed of access 'good' and backing storage requirements and main memory requirements 'reasonable'? A DBMS should help the DBA in this work by providing details of disk activity, memory utilisation, data usage, and response times, and it should identify attempts at breaches of security, program 'crashes', and the use of any restart/recovery routines.

In judging a DBMS, the purchaser should bear in mind the requirements of the DBA, as much as the user. It is important that the users' expectations are not dashed. User expectations should be realistic and for this reason the training and education role of the DBA has been stressed. Users and potential users of the data base need to know something of the terminology, concepts and technology that surround data bases and computing. This 'education' is as important as the 'training' function: how to use the data base system and comply with the standards of the organisation. Users may not see the necessity of moving to data base techniques which may well involve them in a lot of work (some of which may not pay dividends to them but to other members of the organisation). It is frequently difficult for people in one department to have an organisation-wide perspective.

Other aspects of data sharing include the privacy, security and integrity of the data base. The protection of data on the data base is normally the responsibility of the DBA. On liaising with the user, the DBA may implement privacy locks at the logical file, record, or item level. This should ensure that the data is not accessed by unauthorised users. The DBA may be regarded as the custodian of personal data, as required by government legislation relating to privacy and data bases. Privacy locks may also be included to protect the organisation from unwarranted access of the data base by competitors. The encryption of sensitive data may be necessary. The data will be coded before storage and decoded for valid users. As for integrity, the DBA must be satisfied that any application programs are fully tested and corrected before a system is integrated into the data base environment.

The DBA may set standards for copying files. Rapid recovery from failure is essential where a number of users need access to the data base. Recovery from system breakdown can be affected in a number of ways. Before changes are made to data, a copy can be taken which will remain until the change has been successfully executed. More general backup is achieved through:

(a) a complete dump and

(b) a log (or journal file) giving details of any changes made since the dump was made.

Recovery is usually made by 'roll forward' techniques, where the copy is loaded (ensuring a further copy is retained) and the log used to bring the data base back to its state immediately preceding the failure. If the failure affected only a few items on the data base, recovery can be made by 'roll back'. Here the log is used to copy the 'before images' (the values of the affected items before the system failed). In either case, steps will have to be made to ensure that the failure will not be repeated. In particularly sensitive areas, where failure of the system could not be tolerated, the whole computer configuration is duplicated so that if one system fails, due to a hardware fault, all operations can be immediately transferred to a second computer system.

Although some writers argue that it is the users' job to ensure the accuracy of any data admitted on the data base, and that the DBA team need only concern themselves with its security, it is more usual for the DBA to set standards for data validation which will help to maintain the integrity of the data base. This is reasonable because data created by one user may be used by others. Without the DBA, there will be no incentive, or security net, to ensure that the data is correctly validated.

Much of the information about the data base, the data dictionary, and the activities of their users will be documented by the DBA. Even though documentation is not a popular task, it is essential that it is done, and it is done well. It must be up-to-date, so that changes are reflected in the documentation. Some documentation will be aimed at the user departments, others at the programmers, and others at the DBA team.

10.2 BENEFITS OF DATA BASE ADMINISTRATION

Should the many roles of the data base administrator discussed in section 10.1 be fulfilled, then a number of benefits should result to the organisation:

1. New applications will be easier to integrate into the data base. As a consequence, program development time will be reduced.

2. The DBA will be expected to keep abreast of advances in the technology. New technology can be implemented with minimum disturbance to the users. Faster discs or new software may sometimes be implemented without the knowledge of the users (except in better access times).

3. Information on data base contents and use will be easier to obtain. Reports on these aspects of the data base could be standardised.

4. Communication between departments can be improved as terminology relating to data base use becomes familiar to all users.

5. The user and applications programmers need only concern themselves with logical data structures. The DBA will ensure the accuracy and appropriateness of the physical data structures.

6. As the many users of the data base use the same physical data base, the overheads concerned with maintaining the data will be reduced.

7. The DBA may act as representative of the government and society at large, ensuring that privacy requirements attached to personal data are adhered to.

Of course many of these advantages are associated with the use of the data base management system and the data dictionary system as well as the data base administrator. The full gains of a data base environment can only be attained where all three aspects are present.

The preceding discussion on the benefits of a DBA has been somewhat idealistic. It would be difficult and expensive for organisations to recruit a DBA team which successfully performed all the roles covered. Most installations compromise.

10.3 THE POSITION OF THE DBA IN THE ORGANISATION

According to Gillinson (1982), about three-quarters of DBMS installations bought a DBMS before employing a DBA. Yet we have argued that the DBA should play a major part in the acquisition of a DBMS. Further, in some organisations the DBA role is carried out by one person. In these circumstances only a few aspects of the role described in the previous sections could be carried out. In more enlightened organisations, however, the function is carried out by a group of people, sometimes forming a separate department.

In some organisations the position of the DBA team in the organisation is that shown in Fig. 10.1. The DBA function is seen as separate from the Data Processing Department. In view of the managerial aspects of the role, this is certainly desirable. The DBA function should not be perceived as purely the concern of the technical and computer area.

More commonly the DBA function *is* carried out as part of the Data Processing (or Management Services) Department. The DBA may be given managerial-level responsibilities without the status to carry them out. The results are that the DBA reacts to things, for example poor performance or lost data, rather than formulate and carry out policy.

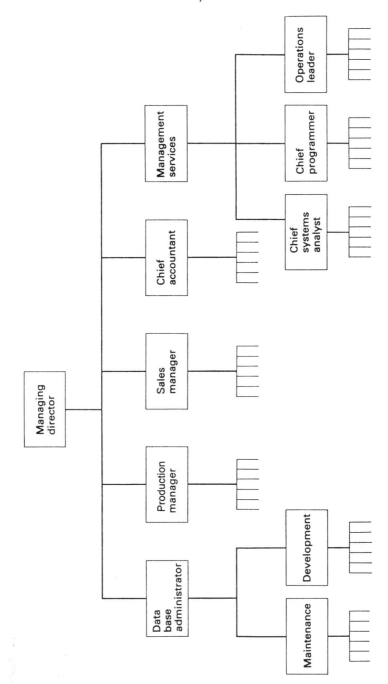

Fig. 10.1. The position of the data base administrator.

Many organisations do not expect the DBA to have managerial-level responsibilities. They limit the role of the DBA to technically-oriented maintenance and innovation associated with the data base. This is likely to lead to problems because there is no-one of sufficient status to enforce standards on users.

We have also argued for a DBA team with people having a wide range of expertise. However, the size of the DBA group in most organisations is small when compared to the data processing group, frequently of the ratio of around 1:10. Worse, DBA staff are usually appointed late in the implementation of the data base, perhaps when difficulties are encountered, and it is impossible to re-design the system though re-planning with DBA expertise might be desirable.

The concentration on technical aspects and the low status of the DBA may be due to the early stage of data base experience of many organisation. A DBA group fulfilling the roles suggested in this chapter will be costly. As more and more applications are added to the data base, the status of the DBA will rise and the administrative role will rise in proportion to the technical role.

At this stage a distinction may be made between the **Data Base Administrators**, who are mainly responsible for the efficient running of the data base and are members of the Data Processing Department and the **Data Administrators**, placed at corporate management level, who are responsible for the development and coordination of the policies and procedures regarding the 'data resource of the organisation'. Each member of the Data Administrator team may have responsibility for a particular user area and 'representing' the user area. The separation of the two functions is shown in Fig. 10.2. Alternatively, the DBA team may report to the data administrator rather than the data processing manager. This distinction, once found in very few enlightened pockets, is now a feature of a number of organisations with large data bases.

The DBA function or department therefore evolves to an important part of the organisation from a subordinate responsibility within a data processing department. With this increase in status is likely to come a corresponding increase in the numbers involved with data base administration. The role of the DBA may well be evolutionary and its importance becomes greater as use of the data base increases.

REFERENCES

Gillinson, M.L. (1982) 'The State of Practise of Data Administration', *Communications of the ACM*, Vol. 25, Oct 1982.

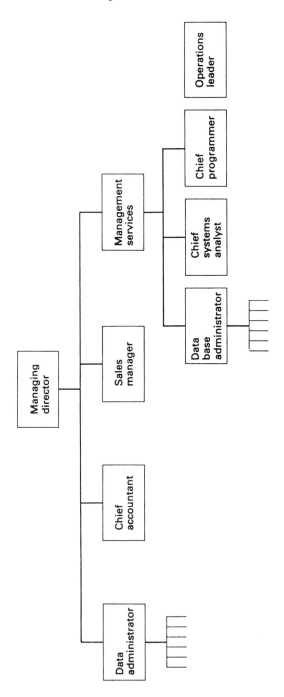

Fig. 10.2. The position of the data administrator.

Lyon, J.K. (1976) *The Data Base Administrator.* Wiley, New York.
McCririck, I.B. and Goldstein, R.C. (1980) 'What do Data Administrators do?', *Datamation,* Vol. 26/8, August 1980.
Weldon, J.-L. (1981) *Data Base Administration.* Plenum Press.

Appendix

An Application of the Approach

INTRODUCTION

The Appendix describes an application of the approach carried out by Aston students in the Systems Development Division of Comshare Limited. I would like to express my gratitude to Comshare for permission to publish these details and to the students working on this and related projects: Andrew Baker, Michelle Chan, Stanley Ho, Kelvin Lam, and Richard Abbot, Sally Beer and Caryn Lewis. The report submitted by the students was 250 pages long, and so it is only possible here to represent the 'flavour' of their work.

Comshare Ltd. is a computer service company. It provides a computer timesharing service (Commander II), software for in-house computers (which could be mainframe, minis and micros), consultancy, and systems development facilities. The software packages include data management, financial modelling and decision-support systems. The Systems Development Division (SDD) is largely engaged in developing systems using Comshare products, which can be transferred to either Comshare's Bureau machine or the customer's machine, once the system is developed.

The project involved:

the analysis of the SDD using the entity-relationship approach to derive a conceptual model,

the mapping of the conceptual model derived onto a hierarchical, network and relational design (logical model)

the implemention of the system using several DBMS/computer combinations (physical model), and

the implementation of some application systems in order to test the appropriateness of the designs.

Obviously, if this was carried out for commercial considerations, only one logical schema design and DBMS would be used.

Entity-Relationship Modelling

In order to derive a satisfactory E-R model, a number of E-R type diagrams (see section 3.4) are sketched from information gained from a requirements specification and from interviews with management. Initially they are more akin to doodles which are then tidied up to use as a basis for discussion. One of the first of these is shown as Fig. A.1.

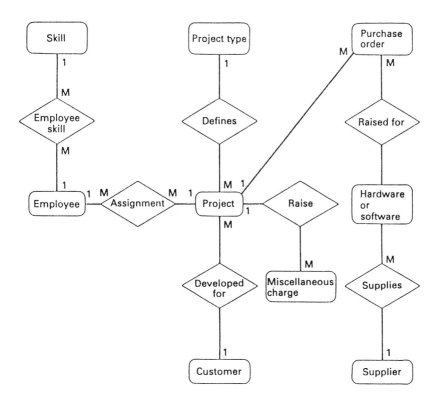

Fig. A.1. Preliminary E–R model for Comshare's Systems Development Division (SDD).

Entities are also listed by name with key attribute but little else at this stage:

EMPLOYEE(*employee-No*,....)
EMPLOYEE-SKILL(*employee-No*,*skill-No*,....)
SKILL(*skill-No*,skill-desc,....)
PROJECT(*project-No*,....)
ASSIGNMENT(*employee-No*,*project-No*,....)
PROJECT-TYPE(*proj-type*,....)
CUSTOMER(*customer-No*,....)
MISC-CHARGE(*charge-No*,....)
PURCH-ORD(*purchord-No*,....)
SUPPLIER(*supplier-No*,....)

Let us see how the E-R model shown in Fig. A.1 was drawn and can be interpreted. The SDD is essentially 'project driven'. EMPLOYEES are *assigned* to PROJECTS and many EMPLOYEES may be assigned to a PROJECT. PROJECTS are *developed for* CUSTOMERS. The CUSTOMERS do not normally produce PRODUCTS (which are produced by Comshare's Research and Development Group). More than one PROJECT may be carried out for a particular CUSTOMER, but more than one CUSTOMER will not be involved in any particular PROJECT. This suggests the three entities EMPLOYEE, PROJECT and CUSTOMER with their relationships being the *assignment* of EMPLOYEES to PROJECTS and *development* of PROJECTS for CUSTOMERS.

Developing the model further, we see that there are different types of PROJECTS such as consultancy, project management, new applications and maintenance. Hence the PROJECT-TYPE entity. EMPLOYEES will have different skills. These will include experience on Comshare's products and experience on different hardware, hence EMPLOYEE-SKILL.

Further, PROJECTS may require HARDWARE-AND-SOFTWARE from a SUPPLIER. (It is not necessary to distinguish between hardware and software.) Normally the CUSTOMER will buy these items but in certain circumstances Comshare acts as a retailer. Therefore PURCHASE-ORDERS are *raised*. Initially, they are *raised* as a MISCELLANEOUS-CHARGE, until the PURCHASE-ORDER has been sent.

After this preliminary investigation of the entities and relationships, further data analysis leads to a 'filling-in' of the detail, and then to an analysis of the possible processes that the data model must support. This was used in the project as a checking mechanism. So as to avoid the construction of a huge data model, and the consequent expense of construction and maintenance of the data base, and the possibility of holding data that would never be accessed, only those data items that are used by processes were included in the model.

In the SDD, a project may originate from an enquiry (an 'event') to the Comshare office from a new or existing customer. Possible projects are discussed in outline with the SDD manager in order to decide whether such projects are feasible. An outline specification is written which leads to the design of the contract between the customer and Comshare, and then its signing by both parties. Each month a summary of project progress is completed by the project manager along with expense details and employees' timesheets. These are just some of the 'operations' following the 'event'. This analysis of functions proved particularly helpful in 'discovering' attributes which had not previously been identified. A revised E-R model is presented as Fig. A.2.

Although an E-R model diagram describes many of the important features of a conceptual model, it does not show the attributes associated with the entity. This detail is represented in the relations, developed from the entities, which are then normalised to third normal form (section 3.7). Thirty relation types, fully normalised, were identified by the group and only some of them are listed below.

> EMPLOYEE(*empnum*, empname, empinitials, empaddress, empphone, sex, marstatus, mobility, nationality, birthdate, birthplace, entrydate, jobtitle, costcentre, salary, commission, lastrvw)
>
> EMPLOYEE-PROJECT(*empnum*, *projnum*)
>
> PROJECT(*projnum*, projdesc, projappl, projhw, projsw, costctr, custnum, projstdte, projendddte, projcost, mandays,...)
>
> COST-CENTRE(*costctr*,cstctrdesc,...)
>
> PURCHASE-ORDER(*purchord*, suppnum, dateorder, datereq, costctr, origempnum, authempnum, totpurchcst)

A further cross-check was made by analysing the report requirements of the SDD and performing an overview document-driven data analysis (section 3.5). Six of a large number of reports looked at were; Project Details, Outstanding Charges for Projects, Office Profitability, Employee Availability, Ad-hoc Personnel Enquiries and Hardware and Software Availability.

At this time it is also possible to start setting up the data dictionary. For this particular exercise the data dictionary was used as a documentation tool only, since data dictionary software was not available. The data dictionary in its final form had five major components:

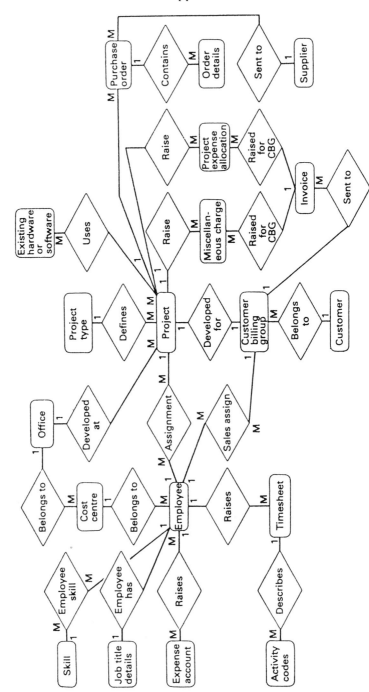

Fig. A.2. Final Systems Development Division E-R Model.

The schema, giving details of entities, attributes and relationships

Functions, that the data base supports, described as events and operations

Physical data base structure

Program documentation

Cross-reference index.

At this stage, only the first of these can be fully built up, along with, through an analysis of functions, much of the second. The third and fourth components refer to implementation, rather than conceptual, information.

The schema definition therefore gives details of entities, which include employee, project, cost centre, customer, supplier, purchase order and invoice, details of their attributes, and the relationships between them, as shown in the E-R diagram. Part completed data dictionary forms are shown in Figs A3-A6.

Logical Schema

The normalised relations developed in the conceptual schema stage form the basis for the relational logical schema. In the relational approach (section 4.2), no links between relations need be specified at the logical modelling stage, they are set up as required when accessing the data base. The model has been implemented on two relational DBMS, Ingres and Questor (from Comshare).

For the hierarchical model (section 4.3), the system ran on IMS (section 7.2). The overall model is represented as a number of connected physical data bases, defined in a data base description. In IMS, and — to be fair — a number of other well-established DBMS, the DBD includes part of the specifications for the mapping of the data base into storage and access method specifications. These physical model considerations perhaps ought to be separate from the logical schema. This overall DBD is split up into subsets which each application program sees, as described in chapter 7.

Sample EMPLOYEE data base definition statements are:

```
DBD NAME=EMPLOYEEDB,ACCESS=HISAM
SEGM NAME=EMPLOYEE,PARENET=0,BYTES=176
    FIELD NAME=(EMPNUM,SEQ,U),BYTES=5,START=1,TYPE=C
FIELD NAME=EMPNAME,BYTES=30,START=6,TYPE=C
FIELD NAME=EMPINITIALS,BYTES=4,START=36,TYPE=C
FIELD NAME=EMPADDRESS,BYTES=70,START=41,TYPE=C
```

ATTRIBUTE DOCUMENT

Form No.	Attribute name	Date	Analyst
A1	Employee number	7 Jan '85	A. Baker

Aliases	EMPnum Emp-no

Description

A unique identifier of each employee of Comshare

Data dictionary name	No. of chars.	Type
EMPNUM	5	numeric (INGRES I2)

Range	No. of occurrences
—	< 500

Validation	Privacy level
numeric	none

Defined in entities   EMPLOYEE , EMPLOYEE - PROJECT

Notes

Ownership: created (Personnel)

updated (Personnel)

reader (any)

deleter (Personnel)

Fig. A.3. Attribute documentation for Comshare.

ATTRIBUTE DOCUMENT

Form No.	Attribute name	Date	Analyst
A2	Sex of employee	7 Jan '85	A. Baker

Aliases	Sex

Description

Identifies the sex of employees of Comshare
F = female   M = male

Data dictionary name	No. of chars.	Type
Emp-Sex	1	Alphabetic (INGRES I1)

Range	No. of occurrences
'F' or 'M'	One per employee

Validation	Privacy level
'F' or 'M'	none

Defined in entities
Employee

Notes

Ownership: created (Personnel)
updated (Personnel)
reader (any)
deleter (Personnel)

Fig. A.4. Attribute documentation for Comshare.

ENTITY DOCUMENT

Form No.	Entity name	Date	Analyst
E1	Employee	7 Jan 85	A. Baker

Aliases:

Description

Gives details of employees of Comshare

Key		Size	
	Employee Number (A1)		176 characters

Attributes

EMP-NUM (A1)

EMP-NAME (A3)

EMP-INITIALS (A4)

etc.

Relationships

SKILLS (R1)   EXPENSE ACCOUNT (R4)

COST CENTRE (R2)   TIME SHEET (R5)

JOB TITLE DETAILS (R3)   PROJECT (R6)

Data dictionary name	Privacy level
Employee	1

Maximum No. of entries ......500........

Notes

Fig. A.5. Entity documentation for Comshare.

RELATIONSHIP DOCUMENT

Form No.	Relationship	Date	Analyst
R1	Employee-Skill	7 Jan '85	A. Baker

Description

Associates particular skills of employees of Comshare i.e. Employee <u>has</u> skills

Identifier

Emp-skill

Employee (E1)
Skill (E10)

Type

m:n

Frequency

—

Privacy level

2

Notes

Fig. A.6. Relationship documentation for Comshare.

Pointers have to be predefined in a hierarchical data base to link the relations (called segments in IMS). Although this means that the data base loses in flexibility, the definition of the access paths implied by the structure means that the paths do not have to be created during query and update processing. The advantage of such early 'binding' is therefore a considerable gain in processing speed and a simplification of query formulation.

The hierarchical data model for Comshare SDD is shown as Fig. A.7. You may note that some entities have had to be duplicated, for

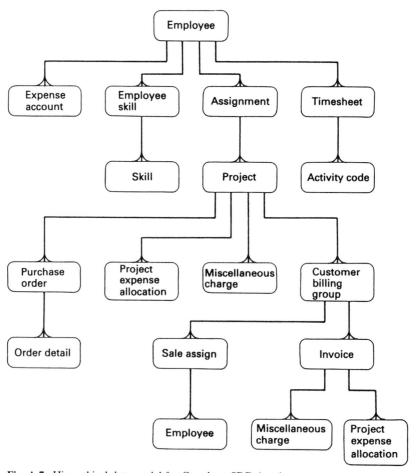

Fig. A.7. Hierarchical data model for Comshare SDD (part).

example, EMPLOYEE and MISCELLANEOUS-CHARGE. This is a consequence of the hierarchical approach.

The network approach (section 4.4) consists of relations linked together in a series of closed loops, called sets. This is a more general structure than a hierarchy. A number of sets are shown in Fig. A.8. The relationship between PROJECT and EMPLOYEE, being a many-to-many relationship is connected by the link record assignment.

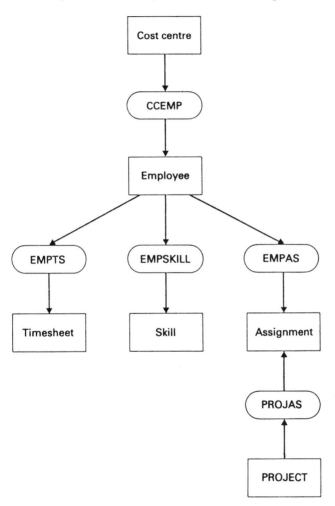

Fig. A.8. Network data model for Comshare SDD (part).

An example from an IDMS (section 7.3) data definition is:

```
SCHEMA NAME IS COMSHARE
AREA NAME IS EMPLOYEE-AREA
RECORD NAME IS EMPLOYEE
      LOCATION MODE IS DIRECT EMPNUM
            DUPLICATES ARE NOT ALLOWED
      WITHIN EMPLOYEE-AREA.

      02    EMPNUM          PIC 9(5).
      02    EMPNAME         PIC X(30).
      02    EMPINITIALS     PIC X(4).
      02    EMPADDRESS      PIC X(70).

SET NAME IS EMPSKILL
      ORDER IS SORTED BY DEFINED KEYS
      OWNER IS EMPLOYEE
      MEMBER IS EMP-SKILL
            MANDATORY AUTOMATIC
      KEY IS ASCENDING EMPNUM IN EMPLOYEE
```

Physical Schema

We describe the implementation using the Ingres DBMS (section 7.5). The data base is implemented on an NCR Tower 'supermicrocomputer' system. After following the protocols of the computer system, the data base is created by:

CREATEDB Baker

Ingres is invoked by entering Ingres followed by the name of the data base, thus:

INGRES Baker

Ingres is then loaded onto the computer system and, when ready, the user receives the message GO followed by the Ingres prompt, *, which indicates that the system is awaiting user commands:

```
\g
*
```

The relations are set up using the CREATE command:

* CREATE TIMESHEET (EMPNUM=I2,MONTH=C3,
                     ACTCODE=I1,PROJNUM=I2)

* CREATE ACTCODE (ACTCODE=I1,ACTDESCR=C50)

This information should be added to the data dictionary.

The APPEND command can be used to enter data:

> *APPEND TO TIMESHEET
> (EMPNUM=1105,MONTH='AUG',
> ACTCODE=10, PROJNUM=551)

Only one tuple at a time can be entered in this way. The use of the COPY command for building up the data is less tedious as the data is read line by line into tuples until the end of file indicator is reached.

The PRINT command can be used to check the data has been entered correctly:

> * PRINT TIMESHEET \g
> Executing...

timesheet relation

EMPNUM	MONTH	ACTCODE	PROJNUM
73420	JAN	73	551
74791	FEB	73	551
81761	FEB	73	712
57321	FEB	73	551

continue...

Ingres replies 'executing' to say that the request is legal and the system is obtaining the data requested, and 'continue' means that the system has finished the request. A number of relations can be printed off by using the print command and separating the relation names with commas.

A list of some of the relations set up is given as Fig. A.9. This is generated by Ingres. You will note that the system follows conventional relational terminology such as tuple, attribute and relation, which some relational systems have avoided, using the more familiar, but less exact, terminologies such as record, field, and file.

The physical way of storing data, the paged heap, is a list (section 5.2) in which the additions and deletions are made at the same end. This heap can be sorted on a particular attribute by the HEAPSORT command. Heap storage is suitable where the number of tuples in a relation is small. Ingres does offer alternative access methods such as hashing, where a tuple can be retrieved on key quickly, or by using indexed sequential access method (section 5.1).

Fig. A.9. Details of relations on Ingres.

Attribute name	Type	Length	Keyno.
Empnum	i	2	
Projnum	i	2	

Relation: actprojemp
Owner: baker
Tuple width: 4
Saved until: Thu Jan 17 17:31:
Number of tuples: 0
Storage structure: paged heap
Relation type: user relation

Attribute name	Type	Length	Keyno.
Empnum	i	2	
Projnum	i	2	

Relation: compprojemp
Owner: baker
Tuple width: 4
Saved until: Thu Jan 17 17:31:
Number of tuples: 0
Storage structure: paged heap
Relation type: user relation

Attribute name	Type	Length	Keyno.
Empnum	i	2	
Projnum	i	2	

Relation: projpot
Owner: baker
Tuple width: 69
Saved until: Thu Jan 17 17:36
Number of tuples: 0
Storage structure: paged heap
Relation type: user relation

Attribute name	Type	Length	Keyno.
Projdesc	c	30	
Custname	c	20	
Costctr	i	2	
Empnum	i	2	
Projestdays	i	2	
Projestcost	s	8	
Percentstart	i	1	
Likelystdat	i	4	

Relation: projapp
Owner: baker
Tuple width: 21
Saved until: Thu Jan 17 17:55
Number of tuples: 0
Storage structure: paged heap
Relation type: user relation

Attribute name	Type	Length	Keyno.
Projapp	i	1	
Projappdesc	c	20	

Relation: proghard
Owner: baker
Tuple width: 21
Saved until: Thu Jan 17 17:55:21 1985
Number of tuples: 0
Storage structure: paged heap
Relation type: user relation

Attribute name	Type	Length	Keyno.
Projhard	i	1	
Projharddesc	c	20	

Relation: salesassign
Owner: baker
Tuple width: 8
Saved until: Thu Jan 17 18:21:47 1985
Number of tuples: 0
Storage structure: paged heap
Relation type: user relation

Attribute name	Type	Length	Keyno.
Custnum	i	4	
Cbg	i	2	
Empnum	i	2	

Relation: supplier
Owner: baker
Tuple width: 68
Saved until: Thu Jan 17 18:21:52 1985
Number of tuples: 0
Storage structure: paged heap
Relation type: user relation

Attribute name	Type	Length	Keyno.
Suppnum	i	4	
Suppname	c	30	
Suppaddr	c	30	
Supptel	c	4	

Relation: purchaseord
Owner: baker
Tuple width: 38
Saved until: Fri Jan 18 13:27:32 1985
Number of tuples: 0
Storage structure: paged heap
Relation type: user relation

Attribute name	Type	Length	Keyno.
Purchord	i	2	
Suppnum	c	4	
Dateoforder	c	11	
Daterequired	c	11	
Costctr	i	2	
Prigempnum	i	2	
Authemonum	i	2	
Totpurchcost	s	4	

Relation: orderdetail
Owner: baker
Tuple width: 18
Saved until: Thu Jan 17 18:21:59 1985
Number of tuples: 0
Storage structure: paged heap
Relation type: user relation

Attribute name	Type	Length	Keyno.
Purchord	i	2	
Purchitem	c	10	
Quantity	i	1	
Purchnetcost	s	4	
Vat	i	1	

Relation: invoice
Owner: baker
Tuple width: 27
Saved until: Thu Jan 17 18:21:58 1985
Number of tuples: 0
Storage structure: paged heap
Relation type: user relation

Attribute name	Type	Length	Keyno.
Invoice	i	2	
Custnum	i	4	
Cbg	i	2	
Invitemname	c	10	
Invitemcost	f	4	
Vat	i	1	
Invtotcost	s	4	

Relation: jobtitledet
Owner: baker
Tuple width: 14
Saved until: Fri Jan 18 13:30:25 1985
Number of tuples: 0
Storage structure: paged heap

The RETRIEVE command enables users to access the data base. In the example it is preceded by the RANGE statement,

* RANGE OF A IS TIMESHEET
* RETRIEVE (A.EMPNUM,A.PROJNUM).

Other ways of using the retrieve command include:

* RETRIEVE (A.ALL)
* RETRIEVE (A.ALL) SORT BY EMPNUM:ASCENDING
* RETRIEVE (A.ACTCODE) WHERE A.PROJNUM=551
* RETRIEVE (A.ACTCODE,A.MONTH) WHERE
                                                A.EMPNUM >8000.

The latter retrieval will give the following relation, using the data shown previously:

ACTCODE	MONTH
73	FEB

1 tuple

Implementing Systems

The system supports the loading and retrieval of the following information:

Possible and Probable Projects: This report giving this information has the following elements — Comshare Office, Customer Name, Project Description, Project Leader, and estimates of Number of Days, Cost, Start Date.

Current Projects: Comshare Office, Project Number, Project Description, Customer Name, Customer Billing Group, Project Definition, Salesman, Project Leader, Start Date, and estimates of Number of Days and Cost.

Other reports catered for by the system include Outstanding Charges for Projects and Employee details.

These reports can be set up as files in Ingres. Further, commonly utilised sets of queries can also be stored and executed on request. When reports are produced by the Ingres Report Writer system, the data is retrieved, sorted, formatted according to the user's specifications (or generated as system defaults), and written to a file or listed directly to the screen and/or printer.

The Query by Form (QBF) interface is easy to use but as it only gives information on one relation in one execution, requests have to be simple. A final standard interface to Ingres (EQUEL) uses the programming language 'C' which is available with Unix systems.

As well as interrogating the data base, data needs to be changed. Data on the data base has to be modified when, for example,

a possible project becomes an actual project or ceases to be a potential project

a current project is completed

an employee leaves the company.

Systems definition therefore specifies input documents and procedures for changing as well as loading the data onto the data base.

Bibliography

Ackoff, R.L. (1967) 'Management Misinformation Systems', *Management Science,* **14**, pp. B147–56.

Anthony, R.N. (1965) *Planning and Control Systems: A Framework for Analysis.* Harvard University Press, Cambridge, Mass.

Avison, D.E. (1983) *Microcomputers and their Commercial Applications.* Blackwell Scientific, Oxford.

Avison, D.E. (1981) 'Techniques of Data Analysis', *Computer Bulletin,* **II**/29.

Bemelmans, T.M.A. (ed.) (1985) *Beyond Productivity: Information Systems Development for Organisational Effectiveness.* North Holland.

Blackman, M. (1975) *Design of Real-Time Applications.* Wiley, New York.

Bradley, J. (1982) *File and Data Base Techniques.* Holt, Rinehart & Winston, New York.

British Computer Society (1976) *Data Dictionary Systems Working Party Report.* BCS, London.

Blumenthal, S.C. (1969) *Management Information Systems: A Framework for Planning and Control.* Prentice-Hall, Englewood-Cliffs (1969).

Boar, B.H. (1984) *Application Prototyping: A Requirements Definition Strategy for the 80's.* Wiley, New York.

Cardenas, A.F. (1985) *Data Base Management Systems,* 2nd edn. Allyn and Bacon, Boston.

Checkland, P.B. and Griffin, R. (1970) 'Management Information Systems: a Systems View', *Journal of Systems Engineering,* **1**, No. 2.

Checkland, P.B. (1981) *Systems Thinking, Systems Practice.* Wiley, New York.

Chen, P.P.S. (1976) 'The Entity-Relationship Model — Toward a Unified View of Data', *ACM Transactions on Database Systems,* **1**.

Codasyl Systems Committee (1971) *Feature Analysis of Generalised Database Management Systems.* ACM, New York.

Codasyl Programming Languages Committee (DBTG) (1971) Report. BCS and ACM.

Codasyl Data Description Language Committee (1978) *DDL Journal of Development.*

Codd, E.F. (1972) 'Relational Completeness of Data Base Sublanguages', in *Data Base Systems.* Courant Computer Science Symposia Series, Vol. 6. Prentice Hall, Englewood Cliffs, NJ.

Codd, E.F. (1970) 'A Relational Model of Data for Large Shared Data Banks', *Communications of the ACM,* **13** (1970).

Crowe, T. and Avison, D.E. (1980) *Management Information from Data Bases.* Macmillan, London.

Cyert, R.M. and March, J.G. (1963) *A Behavioral Theory of the Firm.* Prentice-Hall, Englewood Cliffs, NJ.

Daniels, A. and Yeats, D.A. (1971) *Basic Training in Systems Analysis,* 2nd edn. Pitman, London.

Date, C.J. (1981) *An Introduction to Database Systems.* 3rd edn. Addison-Wesley, London.

Davis, G.B. and Olsen, M.H. (1985) *Management Information Systems: Conceptual Foundations, Structure, and Development,* 2nd edn. McGraw-Hill, New York.

Dearnley, P.A. and Mayhew, P.J. (1983) 'In Favour of System Prototypes and their Integration into the Systems Development Cycle', *Computer Journal,* **26**/1.

DeMarco, T. (1979) *Structured Analysis and Systems Specification.* Prentice Hall, Englewood Cliffs, NJ.

Dodd, G.C. (1969) *Elements of Data Management Systems.* Computing Surveys, June 1969.

Frost, R.A. (ed.) (1984) *Database Management Systems.* Granada, London.

Gillinson, M.L. (1982) 'The State of Practise of Data Administration', *Communications of the ACM,* **25**.

Gane, C.P. and Sarson, T. (1979) *Structured Systems Analysis: Tools and Techniques.* Prentice-Hall, Englewood Cliffs, NJ.

Hsiao, D. (ed.) (1983) *Advanced Database Machine Architecture.* Prentice Hall, Englewood Cliffs, NJ.

Howe, D.R. (1983) *Data Analysis for Data Base Design.* Arnold, London.

Kent, W. (1983) 'A Simple Guide to Five Normal Forms in Relational Theory', *Communications of the ACM,* **26**, 2.

Knuth, D.E. (1973) *The Art of Computer Programming,* Vol. 1, *Fundamental Algorithms,* 2nd edn, and Vol. 3, *Sorting and Searching.* Addison-Wesley, Reading, Mass.

Kroenke, D. (1977) *Database Processing.* SRA, Chicago.

Lacroix, M. and Pirotte, A. (1977) 'Domain-Oriented Relational Languages', *Proceedings of 3rd International Conf. on Very Large Data Bases.*

Land, F. and Hirschheim, R. (1983) 'Participative Systems Design: Rationale, Tools and Techniques', *Journal of Applied Systems Analysis,* **10**.

Law, D.T. (1985) *Prototyping.* NCC, IT Circle, Manchester.

Leong-Hong, B.W. and Plagman, B.K. (1982) *Data Dictionary/Directory Systems: Administration, Implementation and Usage.* Wiley, New York.

Lobell, R.F. (1984) *Application Program Generators — A State of the Art Survey.* NCC, Manchester.

Lyon, J.K. (1976) *The Data Base Administrator.* Wiley, New York.

McCririck, I.B. and Goldstein, R.C. (1980) 'What do Data Administrators Do?', *Datamation,* **26**, August 1980.

McFadden, F.R. and Hoffer, J.A. (1985) *Data Base Management.* Benjamin/Cummings, Menlo Park, California.

Markus, L. (1984) *Information Systems in Organisations: Bugs and Features.* Pitman, London.

Martin, J. (1977) *Computer Data-Base Organization,* 2nd edn. Prentice Hall, Englewood Cliffs, NJ.

Martin, J. (1983/84) *Fourth Generation Languages,* Vols 1 and 2. Savant Research Institute, Cornforth, Lancs.

Mehlman, M. (1981) *When People Use Computers.* Prentice Hall, Englewood Cliffs, NJ.

Mumford, E. (1985) 'Defining Systems Requirements to meet Business Needs: A Case Study Example', *Computer Journal,* **28,** No. 2.

Mumford, E. and Henshall, D. (1979) *A Participative Approach to Computer Systems Design.* Associated Business Press, London.

Mumford, E. (1981) 'Participative Systems Design: Structure and Method', *Systems, Objectives and Solutions,* **1.**

Olle, T.W., Sol, H.G. and Verrijn-Stuart, A.A. (1982) *Information Systems Design Methodologies: A Comparative Review.* North Holland.

Olle, T.W., Sol, H.G. and Tully, C.J. (1983) *Information Systems Design Methodologies: A Feature Analysis.* North Holland.

Open Systems Group (eds) (1981) *Systems Behaviour,* 3rd edn. Harper & Row, London.

Pressman, R.S. (1982) *Software Engineering: a Practitioner's Approach.* McGraw Hill.

Robinson, H. (1981) *Database Analysis and Design.* Chartwell-Bratt, Bromley.

Rock-Evans, R. (1981) *Data Analysis.* IPC Press, London.

Senn, J. (1984) *Analysis and Design of Information Systems.* McGraw Hill, New York.

Shave, M.J.R. (1981) 'Entities, Functions and Binary Relations: Steps to a Conceptual Schema', *The Computer Journal,* **24,** No. 1.

Sundgren, B. (1985) *Data Bases and Data Models.* Studentlitteratur, Lund.

Tsichritzis, D.C. and Lochovsky, F.H. (1977) *Data Base Management Systems.* Academic Press, New York.

Ullman, J.R. (1982) *Principles of Data Base Systems,* 2nd edn. Pitman, London.

Veryard, R. (1984) *Pragmatic Data Analysis.* Blackwell Scientific, Oxford.

Vasta, J.A. (1985) *Understanding Data Base Management Systems.* Wadsworth, Belmont, California.

Waters, S.J. (1979) 'Towards Comprehensive Specifications', *The Computer Journal,* **22,** No. 3.

Weldon, J.L. (1981) *Data Base Administration.* Plenum Press.

Weinberg, V. (1980) *Structured Analysis.* Yourdon, New York.

Wood-Harper, A.T., Antill, Lyn and Avison, D.E. (1985) *Information Systems Definition: The Multiview Approach.* Blackwell Scientific, Oxford.

Wood-Harper, A.T. and Fitzgerald, G. (1982) 'A Taxonomy of Current Approaches to Systems Analysis', *The Computer Journal,* **25,** No. 1.

Zloof, M.M. (1975) *Query by Example, Proceedings, National Computing Conference,* **44.**

Zloof, M.M. (1977) 'Query by Example: A Data Base Language', *IBM Systems Journal,* **16**/4.

PRODUCTS

Adabas: Adabase Ltd., Derby or Software A.G. Hambourg and Reston, Va.
BIS/IPSE, BIS, 20 Upper Ground, London SE1.
Britton-Lee IDM: Britton-Lee, Los Angeles.
CommanderII: Comshare, 32-34 Great Peter Steet, London SW1P 2DB.
Data Designer: Savant Enterprises, 2 New Street, Carnforth, Lancs.
dBase2: Ashton-Tate, Culver City, Calif.
DB/2: IBM, White Plains, New York.
Everyman: Vector Int, Lower Teddington St, Kingston on Thames.
IBM DDS: IBM, White Plains, New York.
ICL CAFS: ICL House, Putney, London SW15.
ICL DDS: ICL House, Putney, London SW15.
IDMS: Cullinet, Westwood, Mass. or ICL House, Putney, London SW15.
IMS: IBM, White Plains, New York.
Ingres: Relational Technology, Berkeley, California.
LAMIS: ICL House, Putney, London SW15.
MDBS: Micro Data Base, Lafayette, Ind.
Mimer: Savant Enterprises, 2 New Street, Carnforth, Lancs.
Natural: Adabas Ltd., Derby or Software A.G, Hambourg and Reston, Va.
Nomad2: D & B Computing Services, Danbury Road, Wilton, CT.
Oracle: Oracle, 34 The Quadrant, Richmond, Surrey.
Questor: Comshare, 32-34 Great Peter Street, London SW1P 2DB.
RamisII: Mathematica, PO Box 2392, Princeton, NJ.
SQL: IBM, White Plains, New York.
System2000: MRI Corp, Austin, Texas.
Total: Cincom Systems, Cincinnati.
Workbench: LBMS, Newman Street, London WC1.

Index

Words in italic signify names of packages or suppliers; page numbers in bold indicate principal references.